After Dark

T0353136

After Dark

A Nocturnal Exploration of Madrid

Ben Stubbs

Signal

Signal Books
Oxford

First published in 2016 by
Signal Books Limited
36 Minster Road
Oxford OX4 1LY
www.signalbooks.co.uk

A catalogue record for this book is available from the British Library

ISBN 978-1-909930-43-8 Paper

Cover Design: Tora Kelly
Cover Images: S. Borisov/Shutterstock; Philip Lange/Shutterstock
Half-title Page Image: (c) Creative Lab/Shutterstock
Typesetting: Tora Kelly
Printed in India

For Laura, Dante and Frankie

Table of Contents

Madrid's Royal Palace at night (Marcus Obal/Wikimedia Commons)

Author's note

The writer William Dalrymple once remarked in an interview that a "contract of truthfulness" with the reader in travel and non-fiction writing, while rarely explicit, allows the intention of the work to be clear and for the reader to trust the author and the presentation of events.

As such, while I have necessarily edited the narrative within this book to allow it to have a coherent sense of flow and rhythm, I was very careful to ensure that all the events within *After Dark* began at their allotted hours. Some of these chapters, as you will see, continued beyond a single hour as I immersed myself in the city and learned that the structure I live by doesn't really work in a city like Madrid, which stretches and elongates experiences and relies on chance encounters and spontaneity as much as anything as the night unfolds. As a result of this discovery during the immersion for this book, which began as a single nocturnal and insomniac wandering on a hot Friday night in June, it continued in the streets of Madrid for many weeks. I have structured the book as a continuous narrative to allow the story to flow more easily for both the writer and the reader. In addition, all the people, places and events are presented exactly as they happened.

This book involved some ethical considerations, as all non-fiction works do when arranging all the experiences and research one has collected and collated into a coherent narrative whole, though as Amy Wilentz of the University of California notes of the process, "It's a weird act of magic: we pluck up a world, hold it in our hands, and then offer it, often across seas and continents and across cultures and classes, to another world for consumption." Further to this, with the world I pluck up and offer to you, I have made the strongest effort to maintain the integrity of the people and the places I visited within the narrative of *After Dark* as this, at its core, is what the book is about.

You may want to appreciate this journey as an armchair traveller, with no desire to ever walk the streets at night, or you may want to follow some of the paths I have laid out, and some of them are straightforward and logical. Just like the night in Madrid, though, many of the walks I took were circuitous and rambling; they would re-cross the same areas and the different times of night would offer different perspectives. Nightwalking in Madrid is as much a temporal phenomenon as it is a spatial activity. An area that might be alive and busy at one point would be lonely and bathed in a solitary orange light only two hours later.

This is my experience of the city; it is the blink of an eye in the history of this beautiful and complex place, though my hope is that it adds another layer, another lens, to Madrid's many narratives and to what visitors may see, hear and feel.

Introduction

Let the night teach us what we are, and the day what we should be.
Thomas Tryon, 1691

I

Bad things happen at night. At least that's what we're led to believe. It is when the insomniacs, psychopaths, nymphomaniacs and photophobics—those who are afraid of the light—roam the streets. Jack the Ripper sliced his way through the London night in the 1880s. The Zodiac Killer began his spree in California in the 1960s as college students on first dates sought privacy using the cover of the night. The Argentine junta of the "dirty war" in the 1970s would use the darkness to grab victims unseen from their beds before flying them out over the Atlantic Ocean and dropping them into the silent water. It seems no coincidence that Satan is called the Prince of Darkness.

The night is when predators stalk their prey and big brothers scare siblings with stories of bogeymen and monsters in the closet. The night is when "normal" people should be tucked up in their beds away from the uncertainties of darkness and the roaming of the "people of the abyss". The Elizabethan dramatist Thomas Middleton wrote that there should be "no occupation but sleepe, feed, and fart" during the night. Only in 1827 was a curfew lifted in England, aimed at banning nightwalking and its supposedly criminal intent.

The notion of darkness in modern cities is very different to what it once was. It is only a hundred years or so since all lighting during the night would be provided by fire. As we mastered this early technology, we transitioned from the small circle of light from our cooking fire, via lumps of wood dipped in resin for a continuous and mobile light source, to grease lamps that would stink like rotting meat. In a more traditional sense there were also cultures that used the materials around them to make light in the darkness, such as the New Zealand Maoris who would set fire to dried mutton fish skewered onto a forked stick, or the Shetland Islanders who threaded a wick straight through the guts of the oily feathered stormy petrel in order to give them a lasting flame and dependable relief from the dark.

Fast forward to the twenty-first century and we have neon lights, LED lights, electric streetlights, battery powered torches, solar lanterns, glow in the dark stickers, lava lamps, waterproof matches and wind-up survival lights just to name a few devices that help keep the darkness away no matter what the situation.

A. Roger Ekirch writes of the fearful place the night once held before the advent of electricity and streetlights:

> Rather than a backdrop to daily existence, or a natural hiatus, night time in the early modern age instead embodied a distinct culture, with many of its own customs and rituals. As a mark of its special nature, darkness in Britain and America was frequently known as the "night season".

The night season became something that inspired and intrigued writers as far back as the eighteenth century, and in Europe this fascination has almost exclusively centred on the exploration of the dark streets of Paris and London. Restif de la Bretonne, both labelled a realist and a pornographer, or a writer who was "melodramatic, self-obsessed and prone to lofty, moralizing statements," as Andrew Hussey notes, paved the way for an alternative perspective of Paris with his *Les nuits de Paris*— Paris Nights—published in 1789. He would walk the lonely streets in search of all manner of vice, not all such examples either enlightening or particularly morally instructive, though Restif's proclaimed motive was to "uncover the dark side of the city so it could literally be moved towards the light". Eric Hazan writes in *The Invention of Paris* that Restif was the "first to describe the pleasure of night-time wandering in this Paris populated by beggars, whores and thieves and the intoxication that takes hold of someone who has walked for a long while quite alone, and aimlessly, just following the streets".

The development of Paris as a place for early nocturnal travel writing was continued by the influential poet and essayist Gérard de Nerval. In his book *French Romantic Travel Writing*, C.W. Thompson looks at the significance, and originality, of exploring a place psychologically as well as physically in the way that Nerval, Théophile Gautier and Stendhal did. Nerval was one such writer who embraced the possibilities of chance and caprice with his "extreme" nocturnal wandering in Paris, publishing a work on his impressions of the city at night in 1852 with *Les nuits d'octobre*. Miranda Gill observes how "The narrative begins with a *badaud*, or Parisian spectator, acting as Virgil to the narrator's Dante, leading him around the nocturnal underworld and its tramps, labourers, and women of questionable virtue." Hazan also details Nerval's relationship with, and journeys through, the night-time city as he existed "on the edge of madness". An impoverished Nerval was to hang himself in a dark Parisian alley on 26 January 1855, having left a note to his aunt that read, "Do not wait up for me this evening, for the night will be black and white." Charles Baudelaire remarked that Nerval had "delivered his soul in the darkest street that he could find".

Beyond the notion of solely writing about the night time, though, there is something alluring, and even addictive, about immersing oneself within it on foot—seeing things slowly without the safety net of daylight or a fast moving vehicle to allow a hasty getaway. The power and appeal of the act of walking, both during the day and the night, have been discussed by many writers. Tim Ingold and Jo Lee Vergunst write that "Life itself is as much a long walk as it is a long conversation, and the ways along which we walk are those along which we live." Nietzsche maintained that all great thoughts were borne from walking, Bill Bryson writes that life takes on a wonderful simplicity when walking, and Dickens was so addicted to walking at night that he wrote, "If I couldn't walk fast and far, I should just explode and perish."

Rousseau's unfinished *Les Rêveries du promeneur solitaire* (*Reveries of the Solitary Walker*), based in part on walks he took in Parisian before he died in 1778, demonstrated the idiosyncrasies and varied perspectives that could be found by a writer walking through a place at night. Rousseau was not particularly enamoured with the urban setting and much preferred the pleasures of the countryside: "I live in the middle of Paris. When I leave my home I long for solitude and the country…" Like Nietzsche, he used walking as an intellectual stimulus and exercise, as he admitted in his *Confessions*: "I can only meditate when I am walking. When I stop, I cease to think; my mind works only with my legs." While *Les Rêveries* is not

Charles Baudelaire, poet of innocent monsters, engraving by Eugène Decisy (Brown University/Wikimedia Commons)

principally set at night or in the city, it nonetheless embraces the temporal differences that walking and night time allow and it was something that would inspire many other writers in Paris.

It is little wonder that the term *flâneur*—a person who idles, saunters or wanders around observing society—originated in France, identifying those who pound the streets, not meandering necessarily, but looking for stories and anecdotes to populate their walks. The Berlin-born Walter Benjamin was a philosopher and cultural critic who engaged with Baudelaire's idea of the street wanderer from *Le Spleen de Paris* (1869): "Who are those unfortunates, whom evening does not calm and who, like owls, take night's approach as a signal for the Sabbat?" Benjamin explored Baudelaire's city in his unfinished *The Arcades Project*, where he examined the impact of urban life on the human psyche. Benjamin even remarks that "Paris created the *flâneur* type" because of the city's connectedness and the "physical shelter" offered by the busy arcades, gates and old neighbourhoods for those without a place to be. He writes that to wander like this creates a sort of intoxication when one submits to being abandoned by and absorbed within the crowd. The *flâneur* was "a figure keenly aware of the bustle of modern life, an amateur detective and investigator of the city, but also a sign of the alienation of the city and of capitalism," as Gregory Shaya writes in the *American Historical Review* on Benjamin's interpretation and analysis of the urban walker.

In London, the emergence of the walker of the city was said to have begun with Thomas De Quincey, whose drug-fuelled wanderings through London in the 1800s initiated a fascination with drifting through the city streets, both during the day and at night. He was one of the first nocturnal loiterers and much of his aimless nightwalking was in search of himself in the labyrinth of the city. In his *Confessions of an English Opium Eater* (a substance which no doubt altered the way he interacted with the streets) he writes in reference to the knotted alleys and strange streets he encountered, "I could almost have believed, at times, that I must be the first discoverer of some of these terrae incognitae." It was De Quincey's urban walking which helped further establish the image of the *flâneur* across cities beyond Paris.

Many, including Chaucer, Shakespeare, Wordsworth, Dickens and Jack London wrote about the combination of darkness and walking. For Wordsworth, who walked the roads of the Lake District at night, this

Thomas De Quincey, c. 1890, by James Archer (Wikimedia Commons)

perspective created a form of rhythmic hypnosis where his nocturnal excursions allowed him to develop his half-formed ideas into poetry. But there was something particular about the change in the world during the early modern era which drew writers to explore the night in London; as streetlights came into existence, first in the fifteenth century with hanging lamps, and later when five thousand oil lamps were distributed throughout the city to light the darkness, it became a place where the uncharted chaos of the night was lessened. Gas lamps arrived in London in 1807 and in the same era across much of Europe (Madrid's first gas lamps illuminated the central Puerta del Sol in this period); work was extended into the hours after dark as a result and there was now enough reason to push many writers into the streets of their now not-so-dark cities. Matthew Beaumont notes in *Nightwalking* that these writers "used the night as a means of creatively thinking about the limits of an increasingly enlightened, rationalist culture"; they were offered an opportunity to explore and temporarily inhabit a part of their city to which they didn't ordinarily belong. As William Blake, John Clare, De Quincey and the rest were exposed to the "otherness" of their city in darkness it became a compulsion for many.

Dickens formed a habit of walking at night, not only in London, but in other cities as well, his "night walking" becoming a narcotic he had to consume regularly to maintain equilibrium; the "psychogenic fugue" it created allowed him to enter a hypnotic state. In 1861, in London, Dickens couldn't sleep. Rather than spending the night tossing and turning, he got up, went out of his front door and explored his city in darkness, walking until he was exhausted and ready to sleep as the sun came up. Dickens thus became addicted to the night. He would walk and walk the streets to make sense of things and to de-clutter his mind—everything from strained relationships to developing the plot in his novels. He did this violent walking through the night hours and satisfying this compulsion allowed him to put all these things in a filing cabinet of sorts while the quiet streets passed beside him:

> Some years ago, a temporary inability to sleep, referable to a distressing impression, caused me to walk about the streets all night, for a series of several nights. The disorder might have taken a long time to conquer, if it had been faintly experimented on in

bed; but, it was soon defeated by the brisk treatment of getting up
directly after lying down, and going out, and coming home tired
at sunrise.

It was Dickens' nightwalking, described in *Night Walks* (1861), that helped
him understand himself and his city in darkness, exploring the outer
limits of London's bourgeois society and "loitering in its psychological
and sociological borderland", according to Beaumont.

In a place like Madrid, my city of choice, writers and *flâneurs* have
been much less obvious through the years–the clandestine nocturnal
explorations which focused on Paris and London in the past have not
uncovered the same secrets in Madrid. One interesting example of night
literature in Madrid, however, is *Luces de Bohemia*, Ramón del Valle-
Inclán's play from 1920 about a blind poet wandering the streets of
Madrid on his last night alive. It is a tragedy reflecting on the disregard
artists and writers have faced during eras of repression in the city and a
"nocturnal odyssey" of old Madrid which begins at dusk and ends with
the protagonist's suicide in the hours before dawn.

The modern city, whether Paris or London, became both the backdrop
and a protagonist in a literary genre that focused on themes of alienation,
madness and the grotesque. "What strange phenomena we find in a great
city, all we need do is stroll about with our eyes open. Life swarms with
innocent monsters," wrote the aesthete Baudelaire. For him, the city was
a metaphorical entity, filled with meanings and feelings:

> Paris changes! But nothing in my melancholy
> Has moved! New mansions, scaffoldings, city blocks,
> Old outskirts, all for me turn to allegory
> And my dear memories are heavier than rocks.

The urban landscape, especially at night, seemed to offer an alluring
range of possibilities and risks. He was followed by French surrealists
such as Philippe Soupault, whose picaresque *promenades nocturnes*
are described in *Les dernières nuits de Paris* (*The Last Nights of Paris*),
published in 1928. Yet the title of the book hints at something that is
slowly disappearing. Cities such as Paris were losing their alluring and
mysterious blackness and were gradually becoming lighter; due to the
advance of technology and commerce the distinction between night and

day began to blur. Under the glare of streetlights and neon, the writer's fascination with the world of the nocturnal street waned.

||

The Polish social anthropologist Bronislaw Malinowski wrote that "to judge something, you have to be there". While this might be something of a generalization, it highlights the importance of perspective and immersion when writing about place.

I am in Madrid in 2016 and I will take Malinowski's lead. I want to immerse myself within and understand the city from a different perspective beyond my tourist guide, which pushes me along a well-worn path of highlights I am neither interested in nor curious about. Dickens and his nightwalking are also my motivation to see what Madrid looks and feels like after dark. It is a sprawling city with grid-like streets, so I assume that it will suit the *flâneur* type of wandering I intend to begin with. Madrid is a city famous for its nightlife, though this is often limited in the popular imagination to flamenco shows and prescribed itineraries for visitors. "Madrid never sleeps," claims the city's tourism website, observing that *Madrileños* are known as *gatos* (cats). Certainly, there is an abundance of bars, restaurants and clubs, many of which stay open almost all night. There is, though, a distinction between "nightlife" and the life of the night that can be made and this is what I want to explore. I am here because I have friends in the city, because it is the country of my wife's family and because I speak Spanish. These are the reasons I choose Madrid as my place of departure. I have never visited before, though I have some familiarity with the place to help me begin my immersion.

Despite being the capital of Spain and one of the most important and vibrant European cities, Madrid has largely escaped the foreign travelling writer's gaze in recent times. Once it was a place that drew Ernest Hemingway, Gerald Brenan, George Orwell and Pablo Neruda, though this interest weakened during the years of the Franco dictatorship that followed the Spanish Civil War. This is something I want to remedy. There are aspects of Madrid, its people, its streets and its history between the hours when the sun goes down and when it rises again the next day waiting to be explored. Jean-Jacques Rousseau's remark that we are blind half our lives because of what we miss in the night resonates again. If we, writers, travellers and researchers are blind for half of our lives, even in the twenty-first century, I wonder what it is we're missing.

III

I turn the lights out. I'm exhausted from twenty hours of flying. I tell myself that I'll do this exploration of Madrid slowly and I'll let my body adjust first. Already I am trying to order and control things. My body clock is nine hours out and my internal routine is telling me that it is time to sleep so that I can seize the most from the day tomorrow. My mind drifts and thoughts rattle around my head in the fog of jet lag. Did I put the rubbish out before I left? Should I start with the Puerta del Sol or the Museo del Prado tomorrow? My circadian rhythm is off; it is still floating somewhere over the Middle East, yet to touch down and check through customs to join me.

Then a thought hits me. What if I don't go to bed? Why do I have to adjust my body clock so quickly? Is it because conventional tourism implores me to begin with the daylight, or is it because in my working life back home I normally experience life with the rise and fall of the sun? Whether it is Madrid or somewhere else, when travellers arrive at a foreign destination most push through jet lag and adjust their body clocks as quickly as they can to align with the daylight hours of their new location.

The people and noises below my apartment on this summer night in Madrid suggest that there is another life just beginning here, one different to what I am accustomed to. They beckon me to go out now and explore. There are people who live during the night hours, who only head out when the sun is down and the others are heading in.

Life beginning at night is not a uniquely urban, modern sentiment. For many Muslims during the festival of *Hari Raya* the day begins at sunset as opposed to sunrise. This is the same for Jewish people ("And there was evening, and there was morning – the first day"). In other words, first comes the evening and then comes the morning.

IV

From a personal point of view, the night has been a time to lock up and shut down. My wife was abducted from a bus at gunpoint when she was younger in the sleepy hours after midnight in Buenos Aires; my children have nightmares when the world is dark and quiet. Everything good in my life, from weddings to graduations and births, has happened during the day.

In addition to this avoidance of the night, I like structure. I live for routines. I am strict with my kids' bedtime, bath time and meals. I'm organized at work and I'm never late. There is something about colouring between the lines that helps me to keep my head above water. As I have grown older, this order has leached into my bones and without a plan of what next and a "to do" list scribbled on my desk, I feel lost. Structure such as this is much harder to grasp in the dark, and even more so in a city like Madrid, where people do not colour between the lines or worry about appearances in the way I do.

To explore Madrid in darkness I will have to throw all these concerns away. Time is looser when it is concealed by the night. The way *Madrileños* experience time is different to my interpretation. Nothing happens punctually, no one is on time and experiences are fluid and spontaneous. Everything works to a different rhythm here. The possibility of no structure and not knowing "what next" scare me more than a potential mugging or a traffic accident. To embrace the night I will have to accept this. Despite the reputation of the night and my own fears of the unknown, I will walk, explore and meet people who live at night and I will let sleep come later.

V

I open the shutters to let in the last of the sunset and put on my shoes. I grab my keys and press "0" in the lift. I know the Buen Retiro Park is vaguely to the north, but nothing else. I walk outside into the night to begin my exploration.

AFTER DARK

This is the story of Madrid after dark. It tells the tales of retired go-go dancers, poodle-blessing priests, night-time taxi drivers and people who live at the airport among many others. It is also the story of night walks in the city and a perspective of the streets before the sun rises.

Dickens wrote of his walking that it allowed a view of "the restlessness of a great city, and the way in which it tumbles and tosses before it can get to sleep". This restlessness is what I will look for now, to accompany me on my exploration of Madrid in darkness.

7pm: First walk

Cities, like cats, will reveal themselves at night.
Rupert Brooke, 1916

The city exhales; its hot breath flows down the lanes of the M-30 motorway and drifts through the winding alleys of the old centre. It is unburdened from the weight of the day. The heat lifts and shimmers off the roads that lead from the cobbled interior to the congested suburbs. The sun disappears behind the rows of apartments and thick Jacaranda trees; the wind takes hold of the leaves and the carpet of purple flowers in the gutters and sends them off into the night to begin their journey.

The breeze that begins the transition of day into night also brings the people out into the streets. It is summer and the city is enduring a record stretch of forty-degree days, so the relief the night provides takes on extra meaning. The first licks of wind bring people out from their air conditioners, and the softening of the light convinces them to stroll in the cooling air. Madrid sits high up on the now sparse Guadarrama plateau.

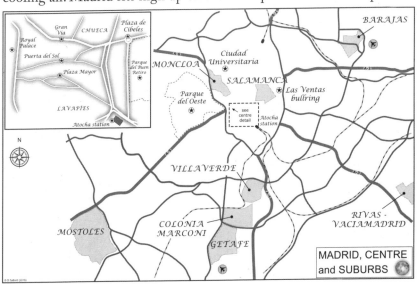

It was once a collection of villages surrounded by forests, roaming bears and packs of wolves. It did not become the capital of Spain until 1561, when Felipe II declared that the government needed a permanent home and a centre from which to command the rest of the country in the wake of the annexation of Portugal and the war with the Catalans. Just as Canberra, Abuja or Brasilia are identified as "artificial" capital cities, Madrid was initially selected for the same reason, as the point on the map that marks the very centre of Spain. The city region is now home to 6.4 million people in the municipality of Madrid. At 667 metres it is the highest European capital, meaning that it endures bitter winters and scorching summers, both of which influence how *Madrileños* experience the night in their city.

As I begin my exploration of the streets I walk without a map. There is something exhilarating about submitting to being lost and not needing an anchor when in an unfamiliar place. I stride up Avenida de la Ciudad de Barcelona full of excitement and adrenaline. People are sitting outside cafés drinking Mahou beers, shops are busy post-siesta, and the pavement still bakes from the recently departed sunlight. I power walk along the wide street under the heavy Jacaranda trees while others stick to the right so I can veer past and overtake.

"Perdón."

"Disculpe."

"Voy a pasar!"

I stride along the path past bars and corner stores. Dickens said he walked "violently" at night. In my uncertainty at what I should be doing on my night walk I wonder whether I should do the same. I cut off a lady pushing a pram as I skip to make the crossing before the light turns red.

"Aye coño!" she yells.

This is the southern part of Madrid. In the suburb of Pacífico the main avenue is wide and tree-lined; the lanes to the side open up to reveal modern apartments and the family-run stores that populate this largely working-class area. Fish shops close their doors and workers in white boots throw the red slush of leftover ice into the gutter. I pass imposing government buildings, cross busy intersections and walk past the former Artillery Park where topless children chase the spurting fountains that bubble up from underground. Then comes the Byzantine dome of the Basilica de Nuestra Señora de Atocha, a church that houses the Panteón de Hombes Ilustres, Madrid's mausoleum for the city's great and good. The complex of church, cloisters, campanile and college stands behind high walls that cast a shadow over the street. Daylight is fading and night approaching.

Matthew Beaumont questions this unusual habit I have developed in his *Nightwalking*:

> Who walks alone at night? The sad, the mad, the bad. The lost, the lonely. The hypomanic, the catatonic. The sleepless, the homeless. All the city's internal exiles.

Beaumont's theory comes from a long history of scorn throughout Europe directed at those who stalk through cities after dark. They are called "noctambulators" and prior to the year 1500, men caught wandering the streets were called "noctavigators" and punished accordingly. If you are alone at night, without a commendable purpose, then you must surely be up to no good. Solitary strolling at night in the city has been interpreted, Beaumont notes, "as a sign of moral, social or spiritual dereliction". As far back as the Middle Ages, nightwalking was a crime. In the late twelfth century the presence of "actors, jesters, smooth-skinned lads, Moors, flatterers, pretty-boys, effeminates" among a much longer list from Richard of Devizes' *Chronicle* highlighted the exotic, picaresque and often unsavoury characters you could expect to encounter if you were foolish enough to wander in the night. This unfavourable view of people who walk at night continues to the present day; in Massachusetts it is still possible to be arrested for being a nightwalker, and you can be stung with anything from a US$200 fine to six months in prison depending on your intentions.

Before the arrival of technology—CCTV, electric lighting, 24-hour businesses and public transport—the night was a time to shut oneself in and lock out the uncertain perils of the thickening darkness, whether they be criminals, prostitutes and drunks, or the ghosts, apparitions and fantasies which evoke terror and fear. Is city life at night still a thing to dread?

Where did this fear of the dark come from? Some psychologists believe that many early civilizations did not fear the darkness, as such, but they feared the perils that arose within the darkness. Thus, night became synonymous with danger and the "instinctive terror" of the night originates with these early people who may have encountered prowling beasts, battering winds or maybe just their own imaginations thousands of years ago. Ekirch writes that night "was man's first necessary evil, our oldest and most haunting terror". Observers as early as Aristotle commented on the fear that night instils in children as young as two, as if it is a question of instinct rather than cultural conditioning. Would our ancestors sit enveloped by the darkness every night, fearful that the sun would never return?

In Madrid, so far anyway, Ekirch and the psychologists seem to be wide of the mark. An old lady sits at an outdoor café chugging a beer, a tanned woman flails along the street on roller skates laughing with her companions, and an army of small dogs inspect the pot plants and garbage bins on every corner as their fastidious owners follow them with plastic bags. Even the streets are now neat and illuminated. The council recently installed 225,000 LED streetlights to minimize dark spaces and to reduce the energy bill of the city. If there is no good occurring, it certainly isn't here.

People in pink, purple and orange Lycra blend in with my speed. They swing elbows, roll their hips and check their pulses to ensure they are hitting their targets. This is also the hour of exercise. During summer there is much more life at 7pm than there would be at midday; the *Madrileños* did invent the siesta after all. Young families stroll past the Menéndez Pelayo Metro station. I'm out of breath and no longer feeling the adrenaline burst which led me from my apartment, so I slow down. This reveals my inexperience too; it doesn't take me long to observe how the people here take *paseitos*, "little strolls". They walk to look at the glow of the sunset in the trees, to smell the frying calamari coming from the *tapas* bars and to listen to the hum of the street without the pinch of the sun. These little strolls are also a chance for Madrileños to display themselves, like birds of paradise, and to check out the *others* on the street: their clothes, hair and accessories, and to maybe hold a stranger's gaze for a moment or whisper a *piropo*, an improvised compliment, while walking and talking with their friends, family or their dog if they can get away with it. Often nothing is expected or intended from these encounters, though it is a common occurrence during the *paseo*. I try to catch the gaze of locals as they walk, though while there are still slivers of light and no darkness to hide my reddening cheeks, I can't keep it up. A woman in a floral dress looks at me from across the street, a man in a muscle top twists his neck as he walks past me, though this casual flirting is not part of who I am—not yet anyway.

Atocha railway station (Jorge Láscar/Wikimedia Commons)

The Avenida is hot; a group of drunken men cycle a strange bar on wheels along the road singing and clapping. One man with a loosened tie and ruddy cheeks stops cycling long enough to knock the top off his beer bottle and he yells at me, "It's much quicker, *amigo*, join us!" I want solitude, though, so I veer through a park near Atocha's grand train station. It is quieter here. A few homeless men are set up on benches and the scene from the edge of the park is a blur of red tail lights from the traffic blending with the hordes of people walking towards the train station. I was expecting dark corners, dirty puddles, lamp-lit alleys and men wearing trench coats. I have read too much, and Dickens, Graham Greene and Hemingway have infected my expectations. The streets of Madrid are clean, the traffic is busy, and murmurs of English, German and Korean being spoken among the *Castellano* Spanish of Madrid can be heard.

I veer right as I pass the enormous pink dome of the Atocha train station, named after the nearby basilica. This is the first railway station in Madrid, built in 1851. Here was where the so-called *tren de la fresa*, the strawberry train, left to travel the short distance south to Aranjuez from where it would transport the annual strawberry harvest to the capital. As Jules Stewart notes, this train was significant as it changed the diet of the *Madrileños* forever, allowing them to include transported fresh produce alongside their salted staples. Atocha was rebuilt after fire destroyed it in 1892—using thick wrought iron arches that resemble the curves of the Eiffel Tower. (Gustave Eiffel was a consultant on Madrid's grand terminal construction, as it happens.) The station was also a determining factor in bringing Madrid into line with the other modern capitals of Europe; soon after, because of the railway, the citizens of Madrid were travellers and tourists like other Europeans on their grand tours of the continent. The first train from Paris arrived in 1864 and Atocha became the centre of a connected Spain.

The station flashed into the world's consciousness again in 2004, when a series of ten bombs, each packed into sports bags with nails, screws and twelve kilogrammes of Spanish-made dynamite were detonated on the *cercanías* suburban train network en route to Atocha during the morning peak hour; 191 people were killed in Madrid on 11 March and it altered the fabric of the city forever. There were more than four hundred people severely injured by the explosions and the only blessing was that the attack occurred at the precise time when many of the local hospitals were changing from night shift, so there was double the number of medical staff available, and largely empty facilities.

The blasts were originally blamed on the Basque separatist group ETA, which had been responsible for many targeted attacks in the city, and this was the line taken by those in government in the immediate aftermath. There were only three days until the general election, and their ability to attribute blame, even without concrete proof, would assist their re-election. The prime minister, José María Aznar, had an intense dislike of ETA and even went so far as to ring Madrid's newspaper editors to assert proof that he would never find. Word got out that the government was using the tragedy for political gain. In the meantime, the police traced the mobile phone detonators from the three unexploded bombs to a locutorio (call centre) in Lavapiés. Shortly after this, al-Qaeda claimed responsibility for the attacks in retribution for Spain's collaboration with the US in Iraq and Afghanistan. This occurred only hours before the election polls opened in the city. The people had been misled and they reacted to the government's duplicity, swiftly voting it out of office. José Luis Zapatero, the leader of the Spanish Socialist Party, became prime minister. Among other things during his term he withdrew Spanish troops from the Iraq war.

Atocha has been something of a centre for terrorist attacks since the end of Francisco Franco's dictatorial rule in 1975. On 24 January 1977, using the cover of darkness, a group of neo-fascists stormed an office near the station where a meeting between the Communist Party of Spain (PCE) and the Workers' Commissions (CCOO), a trade union, was taking place. They had called a strike against the "transport mafia" in Madrid and the *asesinos* were looking for the communist leader, Joaquin Navarro, to halt the strike by force. They didn't find him, so the killers lined up the eight lawyers present against a wall and opened fire. Remarkably, four of the lawyers survived the attack. The funerals and the subsequent protests were the first mass display of left-wing protest in the post-Franco years.

The significance of Atocha from a Spanish perspective and the lingering fear across Europe after the Paris attacks of November 2015 do sit heavily on me. Even though I don't like it, this fear makes me pause for a little longer than usual and look at people on street corners, in groups or "loitering", who I think might be suspicious. The irresponsibility of what I'm doing, walking alone at night and away from my family in a strange place, is also something, which at least now in these early hours of my walking, I find it difficult to ignore.

I will pause and visit the station later in the night to hear its stories in greater detail. Across from the station are the beginnings of the wide boulevard that is known as the Paseo del Prado. Galleries, boutique clothing stores and open, cobbled walking paths leading to the gates of the Botanic Garden line the *paseo*. The Museo del Prado, Madrid's must see attraction during the day, is closing. It contains paintings by Goya, Picasso and El Greco among many others. Up ahead is a statue of the painter Diego Velázquez. He is slouching in a seat looking out to the traffic as if he's about to search in the cushions of his chair for the remote control to tune out the world until the museum opens again tomorrow morning. Across the road is the Museo del Jamón (the ham museum), which can't quite claim the same cultural value as the Prado, though with the specials' board advertising 90-cent beers and €1 ham sandwiches, it is the much busier museum of the two at this time of night.

The white dome of the Hotel Ritz Madrid appears to the right with flags flapping in the breeze; it is another place I will pause at later. From the corner of the Ritz, the uphill slope takes me past the churches and little *plazas* on the edge of the museum. The streets are all well lit; this doesn't feel like I had imagined nightwalking would be; there is no real uncertainty yet, so I head for the darkness in some sort of voyeuristic hope of at least encountering it on the periphery. Across the busy Calle de Alfonso XII the gravel path leads into the trees and the shadowed corners of the Parque del Buen Retiro.

This 350-acre green lung in the centre of the city is as beautiful as any park in Europe during the day, though at night it is the enveloping silence and the outlines of the enormous trees concealing the people within which draw visitors inside. Birds nestle in the branches and rabbits clump along the winding paths lit by the golden glow of street lamps. It is the first time I feel a sense of what the night might be here.

Felipe IV created the Retiro as a royal retreat in the seventeenth century. In an era when Madrid was teeming with sewage in the streets and without proper drainage, it would literally have been a breath of fresh air for the nobility. The park was off limits to the unhygienic public until 1868, long after Felipe's death. Felipe was a flamboyant ruler who, rumour had it, had a nun as a mistress in the San Placido convent across town (an early example of nightwalking in the city perhaps?). Felipe is better known for his legacy of grand architectural projects in the city, including the *Casón* or pleasure palace in the Retiro. He instituted the *fiesta* in Spanish life, in which Spaniards would celebrate everything from birthdays and saints' days to political turmoil. More telling of Felipe's influence, though, was his place at the tail end of the Habsburg gene pool. This line of Spanish royalty had descended since roughly 1500 from one woman, the aptly named, Juana La Loca or Juana the Crazy. Felipe's son, Carlos, brought an end to the line when the family's inbreeding had rendered him unable to stand erect and his mammoth jaw and enormous tongue meant he could barely talk or chew.

Royalty presides over Spain once again, after it was reinstated in 1975 post-Franco. Juan Carlos I assumed the role of the head of state as the monarch nominated to take power by Franco himself. This was always a controversial succession as Juan Carlos appeared to be a keen Franco supporter and he was called by some the "son he had never had". The continuation of the Francoist era was not to be, however, as Juan Carlos demonstrated his intentions once he had been sworn in. He helped

Spain bring in a democratic constitution, a freely elected parliament and a referendum on the choice whether to have a constitutional monarch. This was the beginning of the *transición* to a new Spain and a generation with hope for the future. Juan Carlos abdicated in 2014, succeeded by his son, King Felipe VI, who is a much more dapper-looking fellow than his Habsburg predecessors. Felipe was born in Madrid and also studied law in the city. The six-foot-five-inches military man was also a member of the 1992 Spanish Olympic sailing team. Felipe faces a challenging proposition being a royal in such a politically volatile country, where the relevance of a monarchy tested both by republican movements and by the controversy which surrounded the royals during the financial crisis—his father Juan Carlos went on a luxury African elephant hunting safari during the recession and his sister, Cristina, was involved in tax fraud allegations at the same time—compounds questions over the continued place for royalty in a country where support is waning.

Today's Retiro is no longer a refuge just for royalty or the affluent looking to escape the effluent; it is a place for everyone. *Madrileños* use it during the day to exercise, canoodle or stroll and it seems to be a place for people to escape into at night. The gates close here at 11pm, though there are still hundreds of people casting long shadows as they walk.

The park is manicured and beautiful. There are clipped hedges, shaped rose bushes, clean benches and white gravel paths. An Indian family uses their selfie stick to capture the view back to the city's winking lights behind a stand of trees that look like marshmallows. Two lovers look for lost change in each other's pockets and there is a tanned and athletic transvestite miming the words to a song as a film crew captures her dance moves on camera, blowing a fan in her face to simulate an exotic breeze in the early evening.

Al Alvarez writes that when viewing people walking at this hour, "it never wholly eliminates the primitive suspicion that night people are up to no good". The writer in me hopes this is so and I find it a strange thing to balance. As a father, husband and a generally introverted person I'm happy when life is quiet and predictable. When I put my writer hat on (or shoes in this case) the curiosity borne from uncertainty is all I can think about. I'm a different person when I'm writing; I want to talk to people, I salivate for stories and I'm curious about dark corners, dead ends and what's going to happen next. The satiating of curiosity, which is the travellers' greatest desire, mitigates risk, I think.

Further into the park there are families picnicking on the grass and kids playing football over the green hills. My own children would be fast asleep at this hour. There is something about the structure of Australian life that forces the night out. Walk any suburban city street in Australia at 7pm outside of the very centre, whether it is Canberra, Sydney, Melbourne, Brisbane or Adelaide, and it'll be largely dead. I look at the kids laughing and swooping around the sandwiches and olives on the rug and I wonder if it isn't healthier to embrace the night like this rather than retreating indoors and keeping the night at bay with sensor lights and rigid closing times. Here there are still cafés open, kiosks sell ice creams and bars are serving plates of hot *patatas bravas* (potatoes with hot sauce) and beer. It is early, especially by the standards of Madrid where they refer to it being the afternoon until 8pm.

I decide to walk and turn, by intuition, to embrace the power of wandering a little more. Behind a row of trees, a crystal palace, half illuminated in the rising darkness by a lake, appears. There are people sitting on the stairs like pilgrims at the ghats in Varanasi, despite the hour. Troupes of track-suited elderly people (or those of the *tercera edad* or "third age" as they're called in Spain) are rowing and cycling on the

The Palacio de Cristal (Felipe Gabaldón/Wikimedia Commons)

Bellver's Statue of the Fallen Angel (Tiago Jorge da Silva Estima/Shutterstock)

stationary exercise machines throughout the park. I follow the little paths and lanes that shoot off from the main, lamp-lit arteries into the darkness. I am lost, completely, though aside from the darkest tracks there are still people everywhere.

There is a mossy bench under a fir tree ahead. Once I sit down I can hear the rustle of leaves behind me, the thump of my heart as it slows and the cackle of birds in the canopy. It is peaceful and I listen to the rhythm of my breathing; it seems louder. Everything is more vivid once the colour is drained from the day.

Into the park further, with the darkness now thickening, Satan appears. A statue of a screaming angel, its feet and hands entwined by serpents, sits in the centre of a fountain, with four *paseos* leading to its now still pool. The Statue of the Fallen Angel is the work of Madrid sculptor Ricardo Bellver from 1877. Bellver was inspired by *Paradise Lost*, and Lucifer, as he is depicted in the dark expanses of the Retiro, is meant to signify "he who brings light to the world", according to Veronica Ramírez Muro. Interestingly, Beaumont suggests that Satan could even be the very first nightwalker and the "patron saint" of the night. Daniel Defoe wrote of the wandering vagabond of the devil in 1726. Even Shakespeare implied that the devil was a consummate walker of the night. The Prince of Darkness was significant as the ruler of the night for both Christian and Ancient Greek societies where the distinctions between night and day represented good and evil, chaos and order, and God and the devil. In the Retiro, Satan is quiet and I am alone, so I decide to continue walking.

The crowds eventually thin and the noises sharpen again in the absence of light. The park loses its defining features as the colours are swallowed by the blackness that I can't navigate away from. I have no choice but to walk. Once the familiarity and rhythm of walking take hold again the uncertainty of the dark recedes somewhat. I concentrate on my feet, avoiding tree roots and potholes on the paths and I gaze up, just to catch the next landmark: a lamp, the view of the cars on the road below or a café in the distance.

After a while, being lost isn't as exhilarating as I had imagined and I feel like I could circle the park until morning due to its size. I glimpse a gate along the edge of the park and half-jog the last few hundred metres to walls and the exit at the Puerta de Dante where the car lights and open businesses illuminate the pavement. It is a strange aspect of the human condition to always want to walk towards the light and I'm not strong enough to resist it yet.

Outside the gates the path leads downhill to the Paseo de Cuba where a roundabout buzzes with taxis and buses. There are no streetlights here and the ten-storey apartments stop the breeze from cooling the hot streets. At forks in the road I decide I'll always turn right until I find something that takes me further into the night. There are corner shops and little groceries run by Chinese immigrants all along the street. They sell cheap *litrona* bottles of beer and everything from suitcases to pizza bases. These "Chinos" as they are called here are a constant in the night of Madrid. The owners speak Mandarin until they have to switch to Spanish and they are often the only source of food, drinks and cigarettes for people after dark.

The road tilts down and I pick up speed again. There aren't many people out on this side of the city. Dickens classified two types of nightwalkers: those who wander, "straight on end to a goal at a round pace" and those who are "objectless, loitering, and purely vagabond". I'm not vagabonding, though I have no idea where I'm going. I decide that I'll jump on the next Metro train I find and continue my night exploration rather than walking in circles until the sun comes up.

In his *Night Walks* Dickens writes of being lost as a child and how his walking took on a different, heightened sense because he couldn't find his guide or where he was meant to be. People became giants, taverns were wicked places and statues outside churches were monsters. In the dark, without an idea of where I am, I begin to understand this sentiment. Alleyways that would be uninteresting during the day now make me wonder who is hiding within; men with hoods aren't sheltering from the wind; they must be concealing their identities, and the streets seem to go on for kilometres when I can't clearly see where they begin and end.

So far, though, Madrid seems ordered and open to anyone who wants to explore at night. I am going to jump into its night gradually. I am not quite ready to shed my tourist safety blanket, so my next stop will be within my comfort zone. I find the Metro and take the stairs down into the tunnels under the city; it is impossible to tell in the stuffy and fluorescent chambers what time of day or night it is. I study the map of red, blue and pink lines on the wall and I buy a ticket on the next arrival, to the Opera station in the very heart of old Madrid.

8pm: The tourists

What hath night to do with sleep?
John Milton, *Paradise Lost*, 1667

The family from Chicago stands awkwardly around the Taberna Real, the Royal Tavern, as they're told the story of *tapas* in Madrid. Dad leans down to the bar in order to seem more comfortable with the situation while he slurps his vermouth. He places a hand on his hip to appear casual, though the bar is too low and his t-shirt is tucked into his shorts too tightly for him to pull off the move. What results is an awkward half-bend where he looks like he's beginning a rendition of "I'm a Little Teapot". It's a strange icebreaker for the benefit of the others, who also don't know what to say to the strangers around them.

The phenomenon of *tapas* is Madrid. It is sharing food, sharing gossip, engaging in real conversation and filling the space with the people around you. As the gaggle of foreigners politely take their olives and wait their turn to throw the stones on the floor, "as the locals do", it is everything they're not.

I emerge from the subterranean darkness of the Metro into the fresh air of the night at the Opera station. It faces the shadowed columns of the Teatro Real, Madrid's opera house within the Plaza de Isabel II in the old city. Tourists sit in restaurants eating plates of over-priced paella while the flashes from their camera phones sparkle across the balconies of the apartments above. The children of Madrid comprise the majority of the population here. Teenagers sit listening to Kanye and Drake from their phone speakers rather than the flamenco and Joaquin Sabina of the older generations. They chatter in Spanish peppered with English words. I overhear "cool", "sexy", "clubbing" in the wind. The boys have nose rings and the same hairstyle as Cristiano Ronaldo. The girls have fringes and high-riding shorts; they pretend to scorn the boys who jump up on the remnants of the walls of Madrid on skateboards to impress them. The Moors first erected these walls after they invaded the city from northern Africa in 711 AD. The invaders called it Mayrit, which means life-giving water, due to the rivers that would have once passed through here, and the name has stuck. I know this because a curious sixteen-year-old in the group wants to practise his English and he recounts the story he learned at school to anyone who will listen.

On the edge of the stairs a lady stands with a sign advertising explorations of the night in Madrid. I feel as if I should seize the night, so to speak, rather than wait for it to appear. I follow her, and like the pied piper, she draws eight other tourists who appear from the corners of the *plaza*. We are going on an "authentic", though constructed, experience, though as John Urry suggests, all tourism is a game in itself and the notion of anything being authentic is unobtainable anyway even if we believe we're involved in something more real because of the way it is marketed. This also highlights something else I'll have to shed in order to engage with the night here. The distinction between the tourists (who are everywhere) and travellers is indiscernible and a largely imaginary difference anyway. Is a tourist one with a map and on a tour and a traveller one with language skills and no itinerary? Travel theorists say that tourists are those who invade cultures often without expanding their cultural horizons, whereas the patient travellers are those who are open to more authentic and meaningful experiences. In reality I don't think there's much difference, though I can't help but feel a little inauthentic initially when I approach the tour group.

The guide, Joy, is American. She arrived here five years ago and fell in love, with a man and the city, and she has become a resident. She now gives tours of the famous *tapas* night-time experience of Madrid. Joy has inherited the lisp of the *Madrileños* as she speaks of "BarTHelona", "Plaza THibeles" and the city of "THaragoTHa". Some say the lisp came about because of the inbred Habsburg dynasty and the royals who couldn't pronounce their words properly. The people decided to incorporate a lisp into their vocabulary in order to not make their rulers feel embarrassed. Imagine a modern population adopting a speech impediment if an American president or British prime minister couldn't pronounce their c's or z's properly. It really is quite noble.

Sharing *tapas* is a common pastime for *Madrileños* as well, despite its popularity with visitors, and on the streets of the city there are always throngs of citizens who are keen to *ir de tapear* (go out for *tapas*) outside the guided groups of tourists. It is not a clichéd experience just for visitors, as one might expect; it is an intrinsic part of the social lives of the people here. Our first destination is the Taberna Real on the edge of the *plaza*. It is dark and decorated with brass fittings, hand-drawn tiles and a long, low bar for people to *tapear* and share the small plates of Madrid.

There are a few stories that claim to be the true history of *tapas* in the city, Joy tells us. The first story goes that King Alfonso X didn't like the way that in summer flies and bugs would topple over into his cup of vermouth, stupefied by the alcohol and the sugar, so he decreed that all drinking establishments would serve a piece of ham or cheese to act as a lid (*tapa* in Spanish) for the drink. The other story Joy tells us comes from Felipe II. Apparently he noticed that all his servants were drunk by the early evening because they would drink wine on empty stomachs when they had no official duties. To remedy this he ordered that every glass of alcohol should be served with food in order to prevent drunkenness on the job. Which story is true, I don't know, though modern tourism is happy to pilfer either.

As we sip our own glasses of sweet vermouth on tap Joy tells us that the custom in the *tapas* bars, for reasons of hygiene and history, is to throw pips, serviettes, tooth picks and shells onto the ground as it is more hygienic than lobbing the masticated mess onto the tiles next to people's drinks. It seems a little Viking-like, though it allows the tourists to begin to relax into the Latin mindset.

Mom from Chicago, with her traveller's shorts and concealed money belt, throws a napkin on the floor. She looks back after a moment and it's still there, so she lobs her olive stone and the toothpick there too. "So strange!" she whispers to her daughter. We eat slivers of *jamón Ibérico de bellota*, from Iberian pigs that are fed on acorns. The ham is red and salty and it is the signature food of the city. The World Health Organization's recent finding on the carcinogenic qualities of ham does not seem to have had much effect here. Our *jamón* is washed down with cold dessert wine and just as the Australian in me wants to order a beer as a chaser we exit and search out the next tiny plate of food.

Tapas bar, Gran Vía (Zarateman/Wikimedia Commons)

We skip down the edge of the Teatro Real to the beautiful Plaza de Oriente, which affords us a view of the Palacio Real or Royal Palace. Oddly, this view of gardens and statues across the open ground is due to Napoleon's brother. While Joseph Bonaparte was the occupying king he had the clutter of churches, houses and buildings removed so that he would have a good view from his palace rooms. We pass the statue of Felipe IV astride a horse (which was based on a sketch by Velázquez), now a renowned meeting point in the city, "below the balls of the horse," Joy tells us. Our route takes us through the busy streets of the centre and along to the square that is the Puerta del Sol. The Gate of the Sun is the true centre of Madrid and all of Spain. A plaque on the ground signifies kilometre zero; from this point every distance in the country is measured. The gate was erected here during the sixteenth-century reign of Carlos I, the first of the Habsburg dynasty, a seventeen-year-old king from Flanders who spoke no Spanish and who also held the crown as Charles V of the Holy Roman Empire, ruling over much of Europe and South America at the time. The *comuneros*, the followers of the Castilian crown and the previous rulers, saw the arrival of this inexperienced monarch as an opportunity. The city was hit with robberies, rioting and full-scale sieges by the rebels (and many of the supporting *Madrileños*), so Carlos decided to build fortifications around the city to protect his interests. On the eastern edge of the newly built walls, a golden sun was placed over the entrance, the Puerta del Sol.

The gate and the Habsburgs are long gone, though the square it protected is now the centre of tourist Madrid. The open *plaza* is busy and bustling; it is full of movement. In 2011, Joy tells me, the square was also the centre of a modern rebellion that brought the city to a standstill; *Ocupa* or Occupy began here as a protest by the *indignados* against the 25 per cent unemployment in Spain, the gap between the rich and the poor and the economic crisis. Thousands came to the *plaza* and "occupied" it to demand political change, which ironically did occur when the government brought in austerity cuts to secure funds from the European Union to bail out the banks. The protestors brought with them a village, which consisted of tents, beds, a pharmacy, a kitchen and various workshops. Their unifying cry was "They don't represent us!" referring to the political elite, *la casta*, who they believed had sold their country to the banks.

In more recent years, movement has begun once again in Puerta del Sol, and while fair and regular employment is still a remote proposition for many in Madrid, the unemployment rate has fallen to 21 per cent. With the emergence of Podemos, "We Can", another populist group led people who claim to want a real democracy for Spain, protest is never far away. Podemos began as the idea of 29-year-old lecturer Pablo Iglesias at Madrid's Complutense University in 2008. He believes that everyone is inherently political and that politics is either something you do, or let others inflict on you. When he created Podemos with his students and faculty members after staging an inspiring *Dead Poets Society* scenario, with his students standing on their desks in support during a lecture, they realized that they could effect real change and that they could believe in their dreams for the country. Their motivation was simple, that any real change in their country, which was suffocating in debt and unemployment under a predatory capitalist system, would only be brought about by the people, not the ineffective and corruptible elite in power who had no real interest in the people. They also engaged with the people as a party concerned with the integration of the discontented and of minority groups within the country, united in a common goal of change. This also struck a chord with those who were reminded of the independence and power of the people when Napoleon invaded the city two centuries earlier, and how the spirit of the *Madrileños* led to his eventual exile. In January 2015, 150,000 people crammed into the Puerta del Sol to hear Iglesias speak, and suddenly this relatively new political movement looked like it could topple the ruling conservative Partido Popular (PP) and its main leftist opposition Partido Socialista Obrero Español (PSOE). In the eventual elections, PP won 29 per cent of the vote and 123 seats, far from a majority in the 350-seat parliament. Podemos brought about the change it was hoping for, winning 69 seats and 21 per cent of the vote, ensuring that the old two-party system in Spain was over and that, in order for any party to form a government, the policies of Podemos and its followers would need to be taken seriously. Iglesias said after the result that "today is a historic day for Spain," referring to the power the people now had to reinvigorate their country.

Joy thinks there are "green shoots" beginning to appear with the unemployment situation in Madrid, though it is early days. We pass the statue of a bear picking *madroño* berries from a tree, the emblem of the city, and the plaque commemorating the city's resolve after the 2004 terrorist attacks.

The emblematic bear and *madroño* tree, Puerta del Sol (David Adam Kess/Wikimedia Commons)

The square is full of tourists and locals, many of whom are eating calamari sandwiches, which are famous in this part of the city, while others watch mime artists and jugglers in great circles as people cross in groups to other parts of the city as their night begins. Tourism has long been one of the industries that has kept Spain afloat during its various financial and political storms. The Franco-era slogan for Spain in the 1960s, when the peseta was devalued and tourist visas abolished, was "Spain is different"—a phrase allegedly first uttered by Napoleon in 1808 after his first defeat by guerrilla forces. The 25th anniversary of the cessation of the civil war and "25 years of Peace" (according to the Franco regime) coincided with masses of foreign tourists arriving in Spain. Tourism not only brought relatively isolated citizens into contact with other people and ideas, but it also paradoxically helped make Spain a more normal country, according to William Chislett. Tourism brought 4.3 million people to the country in 1960 (a 43 per cent rise on the previous year), a figure that has risen to 65 million on most recent figures, while tourism accounts for 11 per cent

Plaza Mayor at dusk (Sebastian Dubiel/Wikimedia Commons)

of the country's GDP. Spain is now the fourth most visited country by tourists in the world, and many of those pass through the capital without really ever scratching the surface.

Along with the rest of the modern tourists in Madrid we continue walking through the winding lanes to Plaza Mayor. Three-storey crimson and cream painted apartment buildings with rusted iron balconies surround the *plaza*; there are 237 apartments in all. They date back hundreds of years to the reign of Felipe III (1598-1621), though they are still inhabited by locals; Joy says that one of her friends has a rent controlled three-bedroom apartment here for €260 a month.

Lamps give flittering light across the square as we walk across the smooth cobblestones. This area was once a lake outside the city walls before it became an open space on the edge of the old settlement of Madrid. It has burned down three times, including the fire of 1631 which burned for three days and killed thirteen people. On one side are the striking turrets of the much-restored Casa de la Panadería, which was where the bakery and market for distributing bread was located. Later it was from these balconies below the coat of arms that the royals would watch the sentences of the Inquisition handed out, and it is said that the torture chambers from this era are still under the foundations of the building. In the centre of the *plaza* is the equestrian statue of Felipe III astride his horse, created by Giambologna and Pietro Tacca in 1608. Such is the compact size of the centre of Madrid that this won't be the last time I cross these stones tonight. The *plaza* fuses the past and the present of the city. At first glance it is grotesque: full of bumbling tourists, over-priced restaurants, street performers dressed as Gandalf and Edward Scissorhands and souvenir stores selling replica football shirts, bullfighting posters and authentic Toledo tiles made in China. But even this commercial modernity cannot destroy the profound sense of history contained in the square.

Felipe III and horse (S-F/Shutterstock)

I let the others walk ahead and I stop to look at the balconies, the discoloured slate roofs and the shuttered windows of the apartments. Since 1619 these balconies have witnessed the evolution of Madrid; the first celebratory bullfights in the city, jousting tournaments, the canonisation of San Ignatius and San Isidro and the stacking of firewood on the central stones to allow the *autos de fe* or acts of faith to take place. The Christian rulers would burn alleged heretics and witches alive while they were tied to stakes here so that the crowds of thousands could watch their flesh melt onto the stones. In 1624 Benito Ferrer was the first to be burned alive in the Plaza Mayor for pretending to be a priest and this continued until the last *auto de fe* in Madrid was recorded in 1784. Joseph Bonaparte formally abolished this practice of the Inquisition in 1808, but the Inquisition itself lasted until 1834 (Franco apparently considered its reintroduction). The balconies here have been rebuilt and have endured fires, coups, bombings and modernisation, yet they still witness the procession of day and night. Just for a moment I think of all the feet that have worn the stones down and all the stories within them. My night in Madrid is just the blink of an eye. The stones will continue to bear the weight of this city long after the people here tonight have stopped walking on them.

We continue down to the winding alleys of La Latina, the Latin Quarter and the oldest *barrio* of the city. It was once the Muslim quarter. Now the streets are lined with bars, there are churches and sandstone towers on the edges of the streets and boxes of bright flowers framing the shops and windows; this is old Madrid. Colourful hole-in-the-wall joints and *tapas* bars are painted ochre and yellow; the façades are decorated with tiles and ornate writing. The smell of frying butter, onions and garlic pulls us past the Bodegas Ricla and El Tempranillo. The path continues below street level and we pass a throng of restaurants that proudly announce that Ernest Hemingway was once a regular patron—Hemingway is one of Madrid's most famous literary expats and¬ he lived in the city for eight months in 1937 as a news reporter covering the civil war. It is his fondness for the food and drink of the city that lingers more than his literary talents here, though.

At La Casa del Abuelo we stop and eat soft garlic prawns in terracotta bowls and wash them down with crisp white wine from Tierra de León while men with loosened ties drink *cañas* of beer and eat the same as us. Later at the Mesón del Champiñon, in the cave-like back room, a thickset man plays a keyboard in the corner and we're served plates of juicy button mushrooms. The space is tight and it is noisy, like every *tapas* bar. As knees accidentally touch and plates are passed from one end to the other of the bar, we tourists can't help but put our guard down a little. Glasses of summer red wine are gulped and our talk is no longer fenced in by the politeness of "So what do you do?" and "What do you think of Madrid?" which restricted our earlier talk. This is the real purpose of *tapas* and, momentarily, it confirms the local saying, "When you are in Madrid, you are a *Madrileño*."

The combination of the awkwardness and the popularity of tourism like this is surprising, though it shouldn't be. Group tours and organized travel in Europe dates back to the eighteenth century and in the post-Napoleon years when Lord Byron began his wandering there were said to already be 2,000 English tourists in Rome in 1818, according to Lynne Withey, and up to 30,000 in Paris. The pull to experience the foreign in a pack is still a large part of the tourist experience. In 2016 a group of complete strangers forms a bond and travels in a pack because of a shared desire to experience something they don't have the time, expertise or bravery to explore independently. We are the 'Innocents Abroad', an awkward grouping of cultural exiles quite similar to the group of tourists Mark Twain wrote about nearly 150 years ago as he explored Europe for the first time. In 1867 Twain bought a ticket on the *Quaker City*, a ship that would take a boatload of American tourists on the first organized "pleasure cruise" of Europe and the Middle East. Twain wrote *The Innocents Abroad* to capture not only the exotic people and places he encountered, but the reactions of this new breed of people known as 'Grand Tourists'. The way regular people, or armchair travellers, experience and interpret the world is what many people find most interesting when reading about travel, or as Twain put it more eloquently, "the gentle reader will never, never know what a consummate ass he can become until he goes abroad".

Later, our path takes us past the purple lights of the Plaza de Santa Ana. The restaurants are full and people drink and laugh on the benches beside the theatre. At one end of the square is a statue of Federico García Lorca, the famous Spanish poet who was killed and dumped in a mass grave for being gay and outspoken at the beginning of General Franco's *coup* against the republican government. Lorca was executed outside Granada in southern Spain one hot August morning in 1936 as the civil war rolled towards Madrid.

Given the openness of the Spanish people now, the story of Lorca demonstrates the distance they have travelled since the darkness of the Franco years. Lorca was a radical and the Fascists believed he did more damage with his words than many others did with guns. He was believed to have been killed "with two shots in the arse" for being homosexual, according to Ian Gibson's biography. Lorca was among the highest profile casualties of the civil war and investigation into his death was off-limits until Franco's death in 1975. Many believe the country's accepting nature is as a direct result of the oppression endured during the Franco years; being gay in twenty-first-century Madrid is a wonderfully unremarkable thing, thanks in part, to the legacy of Lorca. The *plaza* is noisy and full of people. From this point at Santa Ana's edge it is said that there are more bars in the 500-metre stretch to Plaza de Antón Martín than there are in the whole of Norway.

Our band of tourists continues walking through the night. There are other similar looking groups walking between *tapas* bars and following the lead of their guides. Our path takes us up Calle de la Cruz to Casa Toni, a family-run *tapas* bar that specialises in glands, kidneys and liver. The thought of sharing bites of *mollejas*, the fried glands of a cow, with the family from Chicago would earlier have seemed absurd, though this is what tourism does to people. I'm not sure if it's the wine or just my understanding that it doesn't really matter who you share an experience with when you're travelling—seasoned traveller, novice tourist or quirky local—though I'm enjoying the night here and the unexpected pleasure of sharing food and stories with people I wouldn't otherwise talk to. We swap intestines for fried kidneys and speak about Madrid as if we belong here. Another bottle of wine is ordered and people are now gesticulating with their hands, laughing and no longer worrying about politeness.

Once the last sweetbread is swallowed, our farewells are fond, and we promise to connect via social media before the next leg of our respective journeys. Like most tourist encounters, though, it is a friendship which will probably be discarded as easily as we would the olive stones when the next experience arrives. Despite the popularity of *tapas*, I've eaten two small mushrooms, a few green olives, a piece of ham and a gland during our excursion.

I weave through the streets and I am at least a little familiar with where I'm going now in the centre of Madrid. My confidence is growing and I'm beginning to embrace the uncertainty of the night here. I'm not sure what will happen next, though that seems to be the point. I feel like maintaining my momentum, so I head to a bar around the corner to continue my understanding of the night.

9pm: Bullfighting

What I take from my nights, I add to my days.
Léon de Rotrou

"How much does a head cost?" I ask at the El Burladero bar. I am sitting below a giant bull's head that is mounted on the back of the bar in Madrid's Las Letras *barrio*. The bull's black eyes stare off into the middle distance towards the posters of the bullfighters that plaster the walls.

"It was €1,500," Manolo says as he slices lemons and prepares his bar for the night to come. "If it was missing an ear, or two, it could have sold for €6,000."

Flamenco plays from somewhere in the rear of the bar while two women dance together with bold flamenco struts near the door. Guitar and staccato hand clapping from the gypsies at the back fills the room. Manolo is in his forties; he has long, black hair and a thick accent from Cádiz, which makes his Spanish hard to decipher. He pours generous gin and tonics and the patrons sit in one of the few bullfighter bars in Madrid waiting to see if *El Rubio* or *El Niño* will show up tonight.

This bar is completely typical of Madrid and, at the same time, it is also one of the most unique places in the city. Madrid is full of thousands of bars, from grimy cafés serving microwaved rabbits' legs and sour wine to the chic establishments that wouldn't be out of place in Santa Monica or on Sydney Harbour. Manolo wanted to live and work at night and he wanted to be his own boss, so he moved to the capital from Cádiz and opened a bar twenty years ago. The difference with El Burladero is that it is one of the few bullfighter bars in the city that isn't a tacky tourist haunt. More than 80 per cent of Manolo's clients are Spanish and, despite being in his forties, Manolo says that his favourite clientele are the eighteen to twenty year olds. "Young people are still willing to see where the night will take them, to be open to possibilities. People in their thirties come in and they have one drink and then they start looking at their watches. They're thinking of tomorrow and of what they 'should' be doing. They don't live for the night anymore."

Despite this, Manolo has lived from 8pm until 4am for nearly two decades. "I live for this city. I love it. So do most *Madrileños*."

At 12am, he says, they're just getting going. I imagine it to be a life of parties and hedonistic nights. However, he disputes this. "We work during the night to survive also. It's not all romantic. It's just that our business caters for the people out at night. Most people work until 6pm here like everywhere else, though they still go out until 2am. Sleep has a different meaning in Madrid," he tells me. "It's also why *Madrileños* invented the siesta," he adds. "Most people have the concept that they have to go to bed in order to work the next day. We work to live here. We don't live to work. We live for another reason."

It's also because all the bars open so late that they don't really have a crime problem in Madrid, he thinks. Because there are so many witnesses at all hours of the night, robberies and violent crimes don't happen often here. "Except once," he adds. "It was back in '96. We were open late and we wouldn't let a group of five gypsies in because they were drunk. Our doorman cleared them out and they told him they'd be back for him."

"And what happened?" I ask.

"They came back for him. They shot him twice in the stomach and then they just walked off." Manolo says that despite this, it is the *gitano* culture that brings many people to El Burladero. *Gitano* flamenco and bullfighting are two of the cultural cornerstones of the city. If they have someone famous or a bullfighter who wants privacy, as they did with Pepe Reina, the goalkeeper from Bayern Munich who was here at the bar last week, they'll close up and pull down the security doors. "We open a few bottles, bring in a guitarist and a flamenco singer and we play until sunrise."

The bar itself is beautiful. It is a big, thick wooden 'L', which is chipped, scuffed and tattooed with scratches, watermarks and stains. It shows the history of this bar in all its imperfections. Two women with red lips and short skirts are propped up in the corner; they greet the single arrivals to the bar and strike up conversations while placing their hands on the shoulders and backs of the men who come in for a drink. Manolo doesn't say it, though I'm sure this is his doing to entice people to stay for one more. We sit and chat; Manolo doesn't rush or prompt me to drink. The commercial aspect of this place isn't evident; it's also why many people here see the bartender as a friend, confidant or psychologist.

"People come here to talk. Madrid is one of the places where you can go out at night by yourself and still spend it talking until closing time."

Two gypsies arrive as we're talking and they begin clapping their hands to the music. I'd been warned about gypsies and Manolo's own stories have me on edge, though when the older of the two asks if he can borrow Manolo's reading glasses so he can read a text message he has just received, I realise they are old friends. The men wear loose clothing and have an air of unpredictability about them. After he replies to the message (asking him to sing in a bar later on) they sway into the back of the bar.

The gypsies, the *gitanos* of Madrid, divide the citizens and their opinions, Manolo says. *Gitanos* are known officially as the Roma people, though I never hear anything other than the term *gitano* in Madrid. It is possible to see them sitting in groups around the Puerta del Sol with tanned skin and worn faces, begging for money. There are many who live on the peripheries of Madrid also. While income by less conventional means might be on the CVs of many, I'd also been told that mostly there was nothing to worry about and that often a negative assumption paints many with a broad brush.

There are *gitano* populations all through Europe, and while much of the bad reputation comes from the crime, drugs and begging of some, especially in Eastern Europe, it is the music and the transient nature of the people that are more obvious. They identify most strongly with the culture of Andalucía, and many people call them the "real Spaniards" because of their connection with place. Their wandering history dates as far back as 600 AD when they left India and migrated via northern Africa and eventually arrived in Spain in the fifteenth century.

Despite being initially well received (and mistaken for pilgrims), the Spanish prejudice in favour of ethnic purity was not far away. In 1499, the "Catholic Monarchs" Fernando and Isabella ordered that any Roma found without a job for more than sixty days would be subject to a hundred lashes as further motivation to find one. Just as the Muslim and Jewish populations were also forced to "conform or leave" Spain, the Roma who stayed were denied the right to use their language, *caló*, hold an official job or even marry. Undeterred by this, the Roma people did not relent, and through their tenacity and persistence the Constitution of Cadíz finally recognized the Roma as Spanish citizens in 1812. There are now said to be around 650,000 *gitanos* in Spain and integration, at least officially, is encouraged.

One of the most evident contributions to the broader Spanish culture is the flamenco of the *gitanos*. This exotic, dramatic and passionate music has a village tradition; folk songs begun in obscure *pueblos* by singers lamenting the death of a relative, the loss of their freedom or the never-ending struggle against the miseries of the world. It is thought that flamenco began in the late eighteenth century around Seville and Cádiz. While it has now been transformed into a modern and adaptable form, its roots still lie with the *gitanos*.

Gitano musicians (Alexandre Delbos/Wikimedia Commons)

"When people are outside of Spain they are proud of the gitano culture and the flamenco tradition," Manolo announces. "When they're here it's something people avoid." As the poet Federico García Lorca wrote, "The Roma is the most basic, most profound, the most aristocratic of my country."

The night is a place where the *gitanos* belong and Manolo's bar celebrates their traditions, even when everything else in the city is changing.

"I don't know if it was the crisis or joining the EU, but Madrid at night has changed," he says. "It feels like the night in Madrid is becoming a franchise. We survived the crisis, but the city gave up something with that. There isn't the same spirit here that there once was. I thank God that we survived, that people in families have jobs and that we're still a safe place." He trails off as more people enter the bar and shuffle among the wooden stools for a place to sit. "It might be different, but Madrid is still a special place," he adds.

I ask Manolo if he might move away from the controversies of gypsies and bullfights as the composition of the night changes here. He shakes his head; he's happy to preserve these traditional elements of the city, even if he doesn't live for them: "I've only been to the bulls once. I don't love it to be honest, though it's part of our culture," he says.

Echoing something I read from Hemingway earlier, Manolo remarks that the people at the *corrida de toros*, the bullfight, want blood. "Why couldn't it be an actual sport without the death, the bullfighting? They duel and then we see them again the next Sunday to do it all again."

We talk about the death of the bull and the sad inevitability of its life, all while sitting under the contradiction that is the head behind the bar. The bullfights are on late in summer, so Manolo urges me to head across town to catch the end of tonight's event, the *novillo*, where young *matadors* make their debut in Madrid's grand arena. Manolo will be here for many hours to come, so I say "hasta pronto", crunch the last sliver of ice in my glass between my teeth and walk out to the dark lane of Calle Echegaray, which leads back towards Sol and the Metro.

Honor to a Spaniard, no matter how dishonest, is as real a thing as water, wine, or olive oil. There is honor among pickpockets and honor among whores.

It is simply that the standards differ.
Ernest Hemingway, *Death in the Afternoon*, 1932

Hemingway's famous treatment of bullfighting in Spain, *Death in the Afternoon*, details the artistry of the bullfight, though before one takes a romantic view of the form, he cautions the reader about the unavoidable cruelty and brutality of the event. He also warns that it is impossible to understand this brutality, history and pageantry without seeing it with your own eyes. Hemingway wrote of his first bullfight:

> I found the greatest difficulty, aside from knowing truly what you really felt, rather than what you were supposed to feel, and had been taught to feel, was to put down what really happened in action; what the actual things were which produced the emotion that you experienced.

Many visitors to Madrid are faced with a similar dilemma. Bullfighting is restricted on television in Spain, and it has been banned in many countries, though it remains a live, summer spectacle in Madrid.

I take the Metro and get off at Avenida Alcalá. The half moon appears on the lip of Las Ventas, the bullring of Madrid. The terracotta-coloured stadium was built in 1931; the Moorish archways, white tiles and wooden balustrades make it look like something that should appear next to the medina in Marrakesh, though this is the home of the *corrida de toros* in Madrid. Vendors sell Spanish flags, matador capes and posters where, for €10, you can have your name emblazoned below the image of a bullfighter; they're playing to the nationalist audience here. The stands are only half full tonight. There are three flags waving above the arena, the red and yellow of Spain, the emblematic bear scooping berries from the *madroño* tree and the seven stars flag of the community of Madrid.

Despite the relatively empty stadium, the *corrida* is popular in Spain once again. As expected, it goes through waves of acceptance and complete disregard, yet it is the *aficionados* who keep the *corrida* alive, even if statistics show that more than half of the Spanish people oppose the tradition itself. There are now three times as many bullfights in a year than in Hemingway's era (up to a thousand first and second class events), and the popularity of the *matador*, as a pseudo artist, performer and the most macho of sportsmen, is still evident in Spanish society. It is seen as something of a coup if someone is dating or friends with a bullfighter. Once the *matadors* were predominantly from peasant stock and they practised their techniques clandestinely by moonlight in ranchers' bull yards with homemade capes, hoping to get to Madrid and to rise out from poverty. Now there is a level of professionalism and sophistication to the role of *matador* that defies the logic and violence of the event. Many are from wealthy families, are university-educated and come from *matador* lines. There are *matador* schools and many have managers and travel in troupes.

Despite Hemingway's warning and the pages of protests I had read online before arriving in Spain, I'm curious rather than disgusted and waiting to confirm my assumptions. I grew up around a farm, I experienced the life and death of animals, bulls among them, close up, so I'm not one who thinks that the meat that you buy from the supermarket is detached from the snorting and shitting animal in the field, though this is something different. The "sport" notion is one I'm not sure about.

The first fighter I see in Las Ventas is Jorge Escudero, a short young man born in Valladolid in north-west Spain in 1989. The programme mentions that he failed to win any trophies last year, though he did cut two bulls' ears off. The programme also details the stud where the bulls have come from and, curiously, there is a section on the medical staff in attendance, from anaesthetists to surgeons, vets and ambulance staff.

In the ring there is the *matador*, two *picadores* (lancers on horses), three *banderilleros* or flagmen and the *mozo de espada* who is the sword page. These men are the *cuadrilla*, the entourage of the bullfight.

The ritual of bullfighting is highly structured, and this is why many observers highlight its similarity to a theatrical tragedy, where the brute force of the bull is pitted against the brains of the *matador*, though always with the same outcome. There are three acts: the first, the *tercio de varas*, is where the matador sizes up the bull's ferocity with a series of passes and dances. The lancer then enters on horseback and "lances" the bull behind the neck for the first loss of blood. The role of the assistants will be gauged by how aggressive the bull is. The second, the *tercio de banderillas*, is where the *picadores* attempt to place barbed sticks in the bull's back. The last, the *tercio de muerte*, the third of death, is where the matador enters the ring alone with a sword and attempts to finish off the now enraged, and quickly tiring, bull.

Matador observed by vets (Manuel González Olaechea y Franco/Wikimedia Commons)

It's an encounter the bull never wins, though sometimes they both lose. "It is a tragedy, the death of the bull, which is played, more or less well, by the bull and the man involved and in which there is danger for the man but certain death for the animal," writes Hemingway.

The trumpeting of the horns heralds the beginning of the event. The *cuadrilla* enters the sandy circle that is illuminated by stadium lights. The assistants are decked out in glittering purple, yellow, red and black uniforms with black bean hats on their heads. They look like jesters, and their role is similar. The young *matador* is in gold and he waits on the edges as the gates swing open and the bull charges in, balls swinging like a pendulum and shoulder muscles rippling as it snorts and gallops at the assistants, full of aggression. The bull is confused and it slams into the barricade where the men hide, before it trots off towards the *matador*.

Jorge sashays into the centre with his red cape. The bull huffs and charges. He dances with the bull and the crowd cheers as he swishes and sways in and around the animal. More trumpets announce the arrival of the mounted *picador*. The *picador* is on a horse armoured with what looks like two grey mattresses, called a *peto*, and the *picador's* feet are stirruped in tin casings. Jorge steps aside as the *picador* advances. The bull charges and lifts the horse and its rider up on two legs. The *picador* sways for a moment and his feet pop out, unprotected. This spurs the rider into action and he slams his lance down into the flesh of the bull's back as if he is skewering a fillet. He does this a second time and blood spurts down its muscled shoulders as if from a burst pipe. This is gladiatorial. The bull will die. I realize that now. It's now just a matter of how it goes out.

There is a family behind me watching the event and their young daughter asks, "What happens to the ponies?" though her father just shakes his head and implores her to watch. Until the 1930s, the horse would enter the ring unprotected and the angry and confused bull would often disembowel the animal. It was common for six or more horses to be killed, with their entrails spilling across the sand, in one *corrida*. Because of the protection they wear, this is now a rarity, though I wonder if the father knows this. The horse is also blindfolded to prevent it bucking the rider off. The bull charges again and the *picador* disengages as their *tercio* comes to an end.

In the next act, the *banderillas* are brought out. These are colourful sticks with harpoon-like barbs in them. The *banderilleros* run in and out, taunting the bull with shouts of "Hey! Hey! Hey!" to get its attention. As one man yells, another darts in and jumps in a high arc. At the apex of his leap he hurls the two spikes down into the bull's back, further enraging the animal. This happens three times until the bull has six barbs hanging from its body; it sways and swats at the sticks, though they are always just out of reach.

Next comes the most shocking part, the *tercio de muerte*; the third act. Jorge continues to move with the bull and it does trip him up once. I have begun to hope that maybe it'll get to leave a final mark on its *matador*, that the scales of nature might be balanced here. Interestingly, when the bull moves and challenges Jorge or there is a near miss, he shouts "Toro!" to the crowd to recognize the gallantry of the encounter. It seems too forced to me, this pageantry and sense of honour, like they know that this is the only gesture that separates them from men who go to dog fights or take their roosters to cock fights with blades on their talons. Despite this, the technique of the bull is seen as an important part of the event for the *aficionados* and many watch the bull and how it reacts more closely than the *matador*.

Jorge bows to the crowd and he struts as the exhausted bull's tongue lolls at the front of its mouth. It's still a 600-kilogramme animal and I wonder what would happen if Jorge pulled a hamstring during his strutting? He'd be toast. A total of 533 *matadors* have died in the ring over the past 300 years. It's probably more than have died from shark attacks in the world during that time, though a fraction of the number of bulls killed, which would surely be in the hundreds of thousands.

Jorge takes a thin blade from the side of the ring and circles the bull. They both pause and breathe, watching and waiting for the next move. Jorge lines the sword up over his head and darts in as the bull charges him. He bounces off the bull's nose as they collide; Jorge sticks the lance straight into the bull's back, up to the hilt.

The crowd applauds and the bull stands for a moment. Is it in shock? The animal slowly, unavoidably falls to its knees. The fight, the dance, is over. The assistant runs in with a thin *puntilla* blade and he punches down behind the bull's head, which drops to the blood-covered sand seconds later. It is dead. This isn't euthanasia; it's like a bully in a playground kicking a younger kid when he's already down. There is technique and precision, though I certainly don't think there is a sense of honour.

In the crowd there are drunk old men yelling abuse at the bullfighter, "Vale, coño! Tenes miedo?"
"Una mierda Chaval!"

They're not happy with the fighter's prolonged taunting and the messiness of the death at the end. This puzzles me. Everyone is here for the dance and the death, though if it doesn't happen in the right way, in the simplest way, as Hemingway noted, then it lacks the honour that the crowd needs, to accept the death they have just been party to and that seems to preserve the precarious place of the bullfight in Spanish society.

Once the bull is dead, the entourage bows to the crowd and leaves. A group of decorated donkeys trot in and they are harnessed to the dead animal. As they drag it towards the gate it sweeps a path of dirt and blood across the arena. Its head thumps on the sand, tongue out and nose full of gunk. It resembles a soiled futon, flat and heavy, staining the dirt crimson as it is lugged off stage and to the local butcher. The lifelessness of the bull while it is removed is the most shocking part of the event for me; it confirms the finality of the act.

I am struck by another comment from Hemingway while I am watching: that people either identify most strongly with animals (the "almost professional lovers of dogs and other beasts" he calls it) or they identify more strongly with humans. "Animalarians" or "humanitarians": this seems an interesting riddle to consider from the stands of the *novillo*. There are tourists in the crowd who are sick at the sight of the blood and the cornering of the bull, there are those who only look at the event through their viewfinder, using it as some strange voyeuristic barrier, like the people who are happy to watch atrocities in their Twitter feeds and beheadings on YouTube, though have no "real'" engagement with the acts. Then there are the old men who smoke cigars and yell at the bullfighters; I guess that they were hoping for a goring or something to wipe the cockiness from the young matador's gait.

There are also many families at the bullfight. In particular, there are many grandfathers sitting with their young grandsons on the hard benches. They whisper in their ears and explain what is happening. The children look on, not scared or disgusted, but sometimes inquisitive or else even bored. The PlayStation version of bullfighting would hold more interest for the kids if it existed, I'm sure. Bullfighting is much more sanitized than it used to be; in medieval Spain bulls were coated in gunpowder and set on fire, drowned, and catapulted to their deaths from the top of cliffs. Nonetheless, the *corrida* still contains a form of brutality that is rare in the modern, politically correct world.

Next in the ring is Manolo Vanegas, who is making his debut all the way from Venezuela. He is twenty years old and I find it strange that in some countries he wouldn't be allowed to sit in the stands with a beer while watching an event like this, but here he dances and deals death to a half-tonne bull. I suppose it's not surprising. In Paraguay I once saw a bullfight where a fourteen-year-old with shin pads and a set of red curtains was let loose in the ring. While I'm watching, it makes me wonder whether the younger bullfighters are more successful because of their youthful bravado. Of the three bullfighters in tonight's *novillo* the youngest are the cockier and more confident of the bunch. Perhaps it's a little like ordinary people, who when they're young think they're invincible, with consequences not as real. I wonder if the older *matadors* worry about their mortgages and their daughters' birthdays while they're in the ring trying to avoid a goring. Manolo navigates the *tercios* with flair; he bends his knees as the bull approaches and swoops under the roaring animal. He dispatches the *banderillas* himself and at the end of the fight, the crowd begins waving white scarves and cloths; it is a sign to the watching dignitaries that he should be awarded an ear for his valour. It is granted, though fortunately the ear is not removed on the bloody sand in front of the crowd. It is a transaction that will take place later.

The bullfight is a troubling thing. Browse any Internet forum and you'll see the heated debate it provokes. I am an outsider, though I can see that it is an activity, whether it is a dance, an art form or a sport, where there is grace, precision and poise in its structure, ceremony and execution. It also has 300 years of history, adding weight to the continued place of the bullfight in Spanish society. In addition to tradition, in pure monetary terms it accounts for significant Spanish tourism revenue (with two million tickets sold each year to events and the growing popularity of festivals around the country) and it provides employment through hotels, stadium workers, booking agents and those associated with the events, which is no small thing in a country with so much unemployment. On the other side of this commercial injection are the inevitable cases of tampering, much like we might see with athletes and cyclists trying to maximize their success and durability. Shaving the bull's horns has been a problem in the past; this alters the bull's equilibrium, not to mention the sharpness of its most formidable weapons. There have been many instances of selective breeding, where more docile bulls with less coordination are preferred to the unpredictable and aggressive types, in order to preserve the money-earning *matadors*.

I've heard *Madrileños* say that there is something admirable in the life of an Iberian bull. Maybe it is a result of the financial crisis or the post-Franco hangover, but some men have told me that they would rather live like a prince for five years than as a pauper for forty when referring to the life (and death) of a bull.

It is undeniable, though, that the *corrida* is a horribly cruel and drawn out pantomime of death. There is a constructed sense of honour in the way the bull dies, though this is desecrated by the ritual torture of the animal. If this is a dance or an art form, would we accept a similar sense of action in different scenarios? Would we allow a painter to cut a live sheep's throat and paint with the blood, because it has artistic merit? It is easy to stay on the fence and appreciate the history and the cruelty from a distance until you see that final moment of death with your own eyes.

"About morals, I know only that what is moral is what you feel good after and what is immoral is what you feel bad after," wrote Hemingway. All these thoughts float around my head as I leave the stadium. The last bull is being dragged across the sand and the *matador* is bowing to the audience hoping for the show of white cloth from the dignitaries in the crowd, which will allow him to take an ear as a trophy and as a token of his prowess. It does not come and he leaves with nothing but his bloody sword. The moon is higher in the sky now and I have more darkness to explore.

10pm: Muslim perspective

The street at night is a great house locked up.
G.K. Chesterton, *Charles Dickens*, 1906

From the bullfight I walk along the avenue with the crowd, I'm happy to drift without having a destination in mind. Plastic Spanish flags flap in the breeze and tourists compare photos of the deathblows on their phones as they walk. The old men, families and tour groups all disperse gradually, to the suburbs, to tourist hotels and to bed. I'm feeling more confident now and the initial fear I had of the unknown of the night is dissolving. I keep going up the dark street until I'm alone and my stomach directs me towards a side lane. Most cafés here are quiet; a lonely man sips a *caña* of beer while reading a folded newspaper at a bench, a group of ladies sits at an outside table drinking cherry-coloured wine and eating slabs of bread from small plates. I consider stopping, though I'm drawn towards a bright shop sign on the corner. It is the universal panacea for night hunger, as felt by midnight walkers, drunks and shift workers after dark: a kebab shop.

Despite just having been at the bullfight, the emotion of the event has made me ravenous for some reason, as if filling my stomach will suppress the conflicted thoughts I have of the *corrida*. I am the last customer at the tiny place with three stools. There are two revolving cylinders of meat turning slowly in the flames. Khurum is in his early thirties and he is the solitary worker in the cramped and sweat-inducing shop, though he is happy to talk as he prepares my meal. A picture of a mosque is laminated on the side wall along with a calendar of the Spanish football team from 2000. I tell Khurum that I am Australian and he reveals that he is Pakistani and is one of the many religious refugees who have been admitted into Spain.

"If I stayed in Pakistan I would have been killed," he says as he slices slivers of beef and chicken from the spinning balls of *carne* onto my plate. The smell of the fat, the spices and the night fill the hot hole-in-the-wall. I drink a can of *Aquarius*, the local lemon drink, to relieve the heat coming from the flames, though Khurum is observing Ramadan and he cannot even sip from a glass of water. He hands over my kebab and while I eat it we continue chatting. He is about to close up so he can go to prayers and break his fast for the day. The last drop of water that passed his lips was just after 5am this morning. Just as it is for all Muslims during Ramadan, the month-long fast of the Islamic world, Khurum cannot break his daily fast until after the last prayer once it is dark—which occurs late during summer in Madrid. I am curious about his story and what night means to Khurum as a Muslim during Ramadan.

"Do you want to come with me?" he asks as he wipes down the bench and caps the sauces.

Would I normally accompany a man I just met at night in a kebab shop into the suburbs? Probably not. I have vowed to embrace the opportunities of the night in Madrid and shed my daytime caution, though. Even in a few short hours I have loosened my grip on complete control.

"I'd love to," I reply. He wraps the meat in cling film, turns off the burners and wets the vegetables in their metallic tubs before we leave.

We get into his Citroen and take the looping highways into the suburbs of the city. Khurum tells me he has been in Madrid for eight years. He is from the Punjab in the east of Pakistan and he arrived here as a refugee in fear of his life.

"There is no religious freedom there at all," he says.

Khurum subscribes to the Ahmadi interpretation of Islam. Ahmadi Muslims believe that the Promised Messiah was Hadhrat Mirza Ghulam Ahmad who was born in Qadian, a hazy Indian city on the western plains near the present-day border with Pakistan. The religion's followers believe that Ahmad established the Ahmadiyya Muslim Community under divine guidance in 1889. The community's aim is to revive the same spirit and understanding of Islam that existed at the time of the Holy Prophet, Mohammed. One of the faith's more interesting claims is that Jesus (*Isa* as he is known in Islam) survived crucifixion and migrated to Kashmir, where he eventually died of old age. Ahmad was born with a likeness to *Isa* and he claimed to be an Islamic prophet, and the second coming of Jesus. This is what still creates the most intense conflict with other Muslims. Ahmad preached a peaceful interpretation of Islam and he denounced all forms of modern *jihad* in the name of this faith. It is a religion of acceptance in the eyes of its followers. This belief is the main variation from conventional Islam and this differing interpretation would see Khurum killed in Pakistan, beheaded or thrown in jail in Saudi Arabia and fearing for his life in many other Islamic countries around the world. "If I was to sit in a café and talk about how I believe the prophet has already returned and not as Mohammed, in Pakistan they'd kill me, but here no one really cares," he says as we drive.

In Pakistan the Ahmadi have been labelled as non-Muslim and according to *Al Jazeera*, 245 Ahmadis have been killed since 1984 (and 94 were killed in a mosque attack in Lahore in 2010 alone) in their country because of their beliefs.

"This is why I received a humanitarian visa for Spain," he says.

Khurum's family is still in Pakistan, and while they also follow the Ahmadi faith, they do it quietly. Khurum was particularly active in his community when he was in his early twenties, and it became a problem. Local fundamentalist groups targeted him and they threatened to kill him.

"My parents still live in Punjab," he says. He hasn't visited them, he can't, though he doesn't seem to miss them as much as I would expect. It is his religion he holds highest in priorities. "I came to Spain. It is a good place, I have freedom and I can practise freely."

He didn't speak a word of Spanish when he migrated, though it was the possibility of linking with the Ahmadi community that drew him here. "I didn't know anyone when I arrived," he says.

The Ahmadi community took him in and his boss at the kebab shop is also an Ahmadi follower. Khurum tells me that Spain has a big Ahmadi community and there are tens of millions of followers throughout the world. Despite the misplaced fear of Muslims that was born after the Madrid terrorist attack in 2004, which was claimed by al-Qaeda, Khurum has always felt safe and welcome here.

"Spain isn't Pakistan," he adds. Interestingly, however, as John Hooper writes, Spain became a nation in the wake of religious segregation, much like Pakistan. Just as Islam is essential to the identity of Pakistan, Christianity was once considered essential to the identity of Spain.

Despite this, Islam has been a part of Spain for centuries; indeed, Spain was a collection of Muslim kingdoms for 781 years of its history. In northern Africa, Arab tribal dominion had spread from the Middle East; the Governor of Africa, Musa bin Nusayr, set his sights on Spain, across the thin strip of ocean, as his next conquest. The commander of his advance guard, Berber Tariq ibn Zayed, was sent across the water to invade Spain with 12,000 Muslim soldiers led by the Syrian Arabs. The first place they captured, Jabal Tariq or Gibraltar, still bears his name. The Berbers and the Syrians rode across the plains, driven by military ambition and the same desire for a more prosperous life that still draws people from northern Africa to the Spanish mainland. Their capital would be Qurtuba on the banks of the Guadalquivir (where modern day Córdoba lies) in the place they named al-Andalus. The Berbers defeated the Christian army and enlisted the help of the Jewish population as they marched towards Toledo, the former capital. It was here that Musa joined him and in 713 AD they had not only conquered the fortress of Toledo, but they now ruled across all of Spain.

'Bayad plays the oud to the lady': a late twelfth-century manuscript (The Yorck Project/Wikimedia Commons)

Despite the imposition of Muslim rule there was continuous friction between the Berbers and their Arab overlords. This was not resolved until the rise of Emir Abd al-Rahman who was a descendant of the warrior companions of the Prophet, a Berber and the son of a tribeswoman. He united Berbers and Syrians and in May 756 became "the new governor of this westernmost province of the Islamic world," as María Rosa Menocal writes. It was a victory which fostered a chapter in European culture when "Jews, Christians, and Muslims lived side by side," she observes of the complex landscape of culture, respect and tolerance that was created in al-Andalus for a period despite the differences of those who lived in the south of the peninsula. Menocal notes that during this era the map of Europe required the Mediterranean to be at its centre when the Arabized Jewish population re-invented Hebrew and the Christians of al-Andalus endorsed Arabic art, philosophy and architecture and recognized the value in enriching their culture with the customs of another.

While the conquest to bring Spain back under Christian control would rage for 800 years until Granada was finally won by the Christians in 1492, initially the reasonable rulers affected "an important social revolution, and put an end to many evils under which the country had groaned for centuries," writes Reinhart Dozy. It was during the *Reconquista* that Muhammad I, the most powerful emir of Spain, looked strategically north from Toledo to a small settlement on the plateau. This is where he would build a fort with four-metre thick walls and guard towers spaced along the plateau at forty-kilometre intervals to watch for intruders. This was a desolate crossroads, which Muhammad used as a lookout post and an *alcázar*. In the shadow of the Guadarrama ranges the Muslims built their defences in a dusty agricultural village and it allowed them to repel the Christians. The fortifications Muhammad built at the place he named Mayrit, or waterways, was to become Madrid many years later. This new fortification would be key to the Muslim rule of central Spain until 1083, when it was finally taken by Alfonso VI.

It would be nearly 400 years until the rest of Spain united under a Christian banner and during this time control of the area was wrested back and forth by competing armies. Despite the fighting, there were also long periods of peace and co-existence, and perhaps this has contributed to the religious openness of the modern citizens of Madrid. While the Moorish population was small after 1083, it still had distinct *barrios* and if most of the

Muslim architecture of the city was long gone, there were Islamic ghettos around La Latina, the oldest area of the city, with a butcher, mosque and a cemetery. Madrid became a place for many migrants to start a new life, away from the continual conflicts around the country, and it was this movement that began Madrid's transition towards replacing Toledo as the capital.

🌙

Khurum drives past the inner city townhouses with gates locked and blinds drawn, past the brown apartment blocks of the outer suburbs where people lean over their balconies and others cook dinner inside. We then drive out past fields where rivers slip under the bridges and goats graze under trees in the yellow grass. We pass an enormous shopping mall, which sits near an old silo and fields of olive trees. At the shopping mall, a gigantic, metallic chute extends into the air. Khurum says it is Madrid's only indoor ski slope and it is one of the largest malls in Spain. I see the golden arches of McDonald's illuminated in the dark and I ask if he finds the discipline required for Ramadan difficult.

"Not really. Maybe on the first day it's hard to get used to being hungry and thirsty again, but I don't think about it. It's not a big deal at all," he adds as we drive up and over a bridge that affords us a view of the skyline of Madrid in the distance.

"I think people who don't experience Ramadan make a much bigger deal of the sacrifice than those who do it every year."

I imagine that this is one of the many aspects of Islam that non-Muslims don't appreciate fully from the outside. Because it is dark I pay attention to the street signs as we drive. I'm leaving my own mental breadcrumbs in case I need to get back, though Alcorcón, Sevilla la Nueva and Villa Viciosa mean nothing to me as we exit and drive into the streets of Móstoles, the second city of the autonomous community of Madrid. Móstoles is 18 kilometres south-west of Madrid and more than 200,000 *Madrileños* live here.

Khurum parks the car in a neat suburban street with identical redbrick apartment blocks. We walk along to where a line of Muslim men is entering one of the houses. This is the Ahmadi mosque. Because it is quite modest and their numbers are relatively few, they refer to it only as their mission house. The main mosque for the Ahmadi is in Valencia on the southern coast of Spain.

I meet Khurum's friends and colleagues and he switches from Spanish to English and then Urdu, depending on whom he is talking to; "I still speak Urdu to my friends in Spain," he says as I lose the thread of their conversation. I get the feeling I'm the first outsider who has visited their mission house, though the reaction to my arrival is one of curiosity and they all make sure to shake my hand and welcome me individually. In the downstairs prayer room there are eleven men and boys sitting, with shoes off, on the rugs. They slip on their embroidered Taquiyahh head coverings and sit quietly on the floor. The Quran is in a bookshelf against the wall along with the Ahmadi readings. At the front of the room is a television where a sermon is being telecast from England. A slim man changes the channel so that English dubbing replaces the Arabic for my benefit.

I am introduced to their leader and president of the Móstoles chapter, Mubarik. He has a round, friendly face and he tells me he owns a few clothing stores around Madrid.

"Would you like water or juice?" he asks. I shrug, unsure of the etiquette while everyone else is fasting.

Mubarik nods and a boy scurries upstairs.

"Please sit, Ben," he says.

We listen to the sermon delivered by a white bearded man, Hazrat Mirza Masroor, their khalifa or caliph, who is the head of the international Ahmadi community. He speaks of the value of having strong morals and not expressing unwarranted anger at the way the Ahmadi are treated. All the men sit patiently with their legs crossed as they listen, despite not having eaten all day. There are also two young boys here who must be eleven or twelve years old and they try their best to be attentive, though their eyes keep sneaking across to the strange visitor sitting at the back. When one of the boy's eyes falls on my feet, which still have shoes on, I smile and silently thank him for his prompt while I sneak them off and place them in the corner.

After the sermon the prayers begin. A tall man in white stands, facing the wall while the rest of the group kneel together, all facing Mecca. The tall man places his fingers in his ears and begins singing the evening prayer; it is late, though because of the setting of the sun the Ahmadi Muslims will not break their fast until their final prayer has finished.

The lilting chant of "Allahu Akbar" fills the room as he sings. It is a lonely and beautiful sound and it reminds me of the call to prayer I have heard for years as a traveller and an outsider, though only ever through loudspeakers on the street and from a distance, everywhere from the rooftops of Moroccan cafés to the hidden lanes on the outskirts of Dubai. This is close and personal. It is something that probably wouldn't be remarkable to a Muslim at all, though I feel fortunate to be so welcome to witness this nightly ritual during Ramadan. The singer's eyes are closed as he sways slightly and searches for the Kaaba cube of Mecca in his mind. The other men and boys now take it in turn to bend to the embroidered mats and to whisper their own personal prayers. They press their foreheads to the ground and speak through dry lips to their God. A fan buzzes through the room as these eleven Ahmadi followers pray, and one outsider sits watching them during prayer time. The youngest child has done what he's meant to by offering his prayers and he begins pulling at his dad's belt, though the silent *oración* lasts for five more minutes in the dark room.

At the end of the prayer they say, "Amen." I'm not sure if this is normal in other strands of Islam, though the men slowly get up and sit in a circle, so that now I am the centre of their attention. I still have a glass of juice by my side and I feel terribly guilty that they want to make me feel welcome before they have any thoughts of breaking their own fasts.

This place, a rented suburban house with a prayer room for men downstairs, an upstairs prayer room for the women and a small kitchen and bathroom is so humble; it is interesting to compare it to the opulence of the enormous cathedrals and churches in Madrid and the Mezquita Central de Madrid or the Mezquita de Omar (or M-30 mosque as it is known for its position over the orbital motorway). The mosque is enormous and the largest in Spain. There is something authentic about the Ahmadis and their unassuming display of devotion in the suburbs.

I chat to the men in Spanish and English. They are all from Pakistan originally and they arrived here as religious refugees. Mubarik came here in 1974 from Banian in Pakistan's north and he tells me that Spain is the only place that would accept them all so willingly: "I remember the people in our village boycotted us. We couldn't buy or sell anything or even go to school. Many times people would stone our house," he says. I meet students, a doctor, an engineer, shop workers, fathers, brothers and sons, all who have similar stories. There are now Ahmadi followers in 206 countries around the world. Despite the fact that they are yet to break their fast they bring me another glass of juice while we chat.

The smell of food wafts from upstairs. It is a Friday and they are having a *congreso* all together. Mubarik tells me that tomorrow they'll be having many more followers here, from Morocco, Spain, India and Pakistan. There are also many women followers, though tonight it is just the men.

Mubarik says that he's been back to Pakistan a few times to visit his family, though his children were born in Spain and this is their country now. There are many among the group like Khurum, who can't go back to see their families and friends. "There are still many problems with being an Ahmadi in Pakistan," Mubarik tells me. "Recently an Ahmadi man was killed outside Lahore, and last year an Ahmadi from the US, who was in Pakistan for an NGO, was killed by an anti-Ahmadi mob," Khurum adds. "In Madrid we have no problems," he says.

Despite what happened here in 2004 and the links with radicalism made by the angry or uneducated for all Muslims, they are generally treated with respect and made to feel like *Madrileños*.

It is time to break their fast and plates of vegetables, spiced meat, rice, potatoes, jugs of juice and dates are brought out and, unsurprisingly, I'm offered the first plate of food. I don't tell them I've just eaten a kebab and I oblige before the rest are served. While the relief at the arrival of night and the end of their fast must be great, this isn't a special occasion. It is a normal Friday night and just one night during a month of fasting and discipline. This is the most significant realisation for me, that the reality of an occasion such as this is quite different, and much more low-key, than I would have expected from the outside. With the tide of suspicion directed at Muslims around the world in 2016, experiences such as this are valuable, and should be shared by more people in order to appreciate the reality of life lived by the vast majority of Muslims.

At the end of the meal, the men say goodbye and tell me I am welcome to return whenever I would like. Many have work starting early in the morning, whether they are second jobs or part of their seven-day cycle. It is a reminder that Spain has its own problems too.

Khurum offers to drive me to the nearby train station, so I can return to the city. In the back seat he brings along Sharkeel, the twelve-year-old son of one of the men. Sharkeel has never met an Australian before and he asks me questions as we drive. "Have you read the Quran?" is his first. I shake my head and he doesn't quite understand how this could be possible. I haven't read Harry Potter either, and he's nearly as shocked. We chat about football and Australia until we arrive at the vacant block behind the Móstoles train station.

"Don't worry, just walk into the tunnel," Khurum tells me as they drive off. I scurry across the dark field and up into the deserted suburban station.

The night means different things to different people in Madrid and the perspective I have been given of the Ahmadi during Ramadan is a rare and valuable window into their night lives.

I have decided, reluctantly initially, to embrace the notion of chance tonight, to swim in it. I will wait for the unexpected swells to come along and propel me into encounters within nocturnal Madrid and I will try and surf and stay afloat within them. Australian academic and experimental travel writer Stephen Muecke does something similar in his 2012 *Contingency in Madagascar* where he lets chance encounters and caprice guide the entire direction of his book on the island, right from the very first encounter in a taxi at the airport through to his trips in fishing boats off the coast and conversations with prostitutes on strike. The idea of contingency and chance seems to fit a place like Madrid and also the fluidity of the night, so I will try and relax my grip on the paths I follow, my ideas for an itinerary and let it flow, just as I have with Khurum.

The train back to the city is full of people coming in to go out: fathers with daughters sleeping on their knees and women wearing active wear balancing worn-looking prams against the rails as the carriage rattles back to Atocha. Before I take my next train, I want to stop to look at the monument upstairs at the station. On 11 March 2004 this is where Madrid's (and Spain's) worst ever terrorist attack occurred, when a series of coordinated bombs detonated in the crammed *cercanías* trains in the morning peak hour, all heading for Atocha. Pregnant women, babies, schoolchildren, Christians and Muslims were among the dead. The Ahmadi obviously had nothing to do with the bombings, though as in many places around the world, they are grouped together with the extreme minority of their faith when it displays its most abhorrent side. Despite this, the Ahmadi people continually told me that Spain and the

Madrileños are accepting, open and more intelligent when it comes to matters of religion than anywhere else they've been.

I wonder whether it is because once upon a time, Madrid was known as Mayrït and was a Muslim city long before it began to resemble the place I now see. The Muslim rulers of Madrid reigned in a period that was said to be one of cultural enlightenment and tolerance. Jules Stewart writes of the early Muslim days, "For a brief period, Muslim Spain was the most vibrant spot on Earth, a place that saw the magical fusion of commerce, learning and power." Madrid gradually became the capital and a modern metropolis and despite (or maybe because of) its history it now has a strong and visible Muslim community alongside the more prominent Christian presence.

I snap out of my wandering thoughts as I walk from the platform. Up the stairs I visit the haunting memorial to M-11, as the terrorist attack is called, in the centre of the station. It's late and I'm the only one there, though the lady at the desk lets me in. On the wall there are 191 names of the Spanish and foreign victims. Through another door the air conditioning is off and the hot air sucks up towards a ten-metre clear plastic tube, which is the memorial. Inside the cone there are messages

Messages from around the world (Daniel Smith/Wikimedia Commons)

from all over the world, written in Spanish, English, Hebrew and Japanese among many others:

> With all our love
> Words aren't enough to describe the pain…
> Please leave us alone and let the happiness come into our hearts again.
> Peace
> Freedom

Seeing all this and understanding the difficulties people like Khurum and Mubarik would have faced in the wake of the worst terrorist attack in Europe since the 1988 Lockerbie bombing—on top of everything they have confronted in Pakistan—makes their acceptance of me and their positive outlook even more encouraging. They all commended the Spanish people, who could observe a tragedy like this for what it was: a horrific act of terrorism by an extreme minority. I'm not sure my own country would be capable of such maturity of thought in a situation like this. I buy another Metro ticket while I'm in the station; there is another minority group I'm curious to get to know during the night.

11pm: The airport

It is a feeling of relief, almost of pleasure, at knowing yourself at last genuinely down and out.
George Orwell, *Down and Out in Paris and London*, 1933

Have you ever slept at an airport in between a late arrival and an early departure? Or have you slept on any sort of temporary platform for that matter—whether a bus shelter, the bench in a train station or the doorway of a hostel?

I remember spending the night in Kuala Lumpur's airport before an early flight to India years ago, coiled and constantly uncomfortable on the chairs with my head buried against the flicker of the incessant fluorescent lights. I spent another night at the airport in Milan with my wife before we flew to Morocco. We stretched out on a bench across from a 24-hour McDonald's with no real rest at all before our flight opened at 5am and we could leave. All this was to save a few dollars.

What if you were in Madrid and you had to sleep at the airport tonight? What if saving a few dollars was the least of your worries? Would you find a corner, roll out your camping mat, make a bed and go through your nightly routine, or would you just curl up and shut the world out? What if you had to do this again tomorrow, and the next day and the next until years had passed, just in order to survive? I had read about the people who lived, at night, in the corners of Terminal 4 at Madrid's Barajas Airport just like this so they could survive.

The latest official statistics count 23,000 homeless people in Spain, but charities estimate that the real figure is closer to 40,000. Many of those live, and struggle, on Madrid's streets where the most recent figures from the Madrid City Council reveal around 1,900 homeless though the real number is thought to be much higher. While this doesn't seem like a large number compared to many places, it still intrigues me that those in the airport have chosen to live in this microcosm outside the city and that, by and large, their stories remain hidden. Many of these people exist on the fringes and struggle like this as a result of the 2008 financial meltdown which resulted in part from the subprime mortgage collapse in the US and the fact that Spain had 18 per cent of its GDP bound up in the construction and property market and 20 per cent of its employment in this sector at the same time. The property market concentration in Spain created an environment of overpriced houses, low interest loans and unsustainable tax breaks. When things went bust after the US collapse it led to 5.9 million people being unemployed in Spain with 1.5 million from the housing industry alone—the largest number in the industrialized world at the time—and a crippling debt and a situation where Spanish banks had €470 billion in outstanding loans from construction companies and developers. While things have improved since then after a variety of cost-cutting measures, there are still many people who cannot get back into the system of employment and stable housing.

At 11pm I take the Metro out of the city centre from Atocha to see if it is true that some of the people impacted by the crisis now live at the airport because they have nowhere else to go. The train rumbles through the inner suburbs of Madrid. It is still packed and will be for many hours to come. In my carriage three women sit in a row reading their phones, a boy in football shorts with earphones in is playing a game on his screen and a man wearing flip-flops is watching a film on his tablet. All along the carriage there are seventeen people disconnected from reality on their phones; only one man is reading a newspaper and another in a suit is reading a novel.

I see a man, maybe 25 years old, writing precise Mandarin characters in a notebook as the train jostles along. I wonder if he's doing his homework or just satisfying his curiosity. He has four big gulp frozen cola drinks sitting by his feet. When his stop comes he closes his book as he completes his sentence. He picks up his four drinks and balances them out of the door before disappearing into the night.

I exit at Nuevos Ministerios and walk through the tunnels and escalators to make my connecting train. There are people walking with their heads down, on WhatsApp, Facebook and Skype. So many commuters are disconnected here, and it's not just the locals. The tourists I see are buried in *Lonely Planet* guides reading how they should experience the place. They could simply look up and observe. Part of my night journey to the airport is because I don't want to be another tourist disconnected from what is around me. I want to look through the urban camouflage to see if I can talk to the people *sin hogar* in Terminal 4.

Barajas Airport (Flo Weiss/Wikimedia Commons)

There are more than one million square metres distributed between the terminals at Barajas, one of the largest airports in Europe, so I don't expect to find people as soon as I step through the gates. I'm carrying a backpack and my passport so I can blend in, though with 100,000 people passing through Terminal 4 each day, I have little to worry about. I take the escalators up and down under the bug-eyed silver lights and the enormous yellow supports designed by English architect Richard Rogers.

There are flights to Tenerife, London and Berlin up next on the board and I decide to begin my search on the first floor. I'm not sure if I should head to arrivals or departures, as the people I'm looking for aren't really doing either. I see Russian tourists with white trousers and gold chains changing money, Americans guffawing loudly outside McDonald's as they spoon in McFlurries, and Spanish families trotting off through the security gates on holidays. I can't see anyone who looks like they live here though. What should they look like? I wonder. Would I see them coming back from the bathroom in their robes wearing shower caps, or putting out washing across the chairs outside the Bellota restaurant?

I sit at McDonald's to watch the blur and rush of the airport. The travellers walk with purpose. Tickets and passports in hand, they glance from watch, to departure board and then to the direction of their gates. They are efficient and direct. Women roll designer carry-on bags to security, mothers hurry distracted children along and people eat quickly, looking through the movement of the space around them and imagining where they're about to go.

I see one man wearing old jeans who seems a little dishevelled as he pushes a sports bag around on a trolley. Could he be one of the people who lives here? When I think about it, though, I'm judging him too quickly. I'm wearing paint splattered cargo shorts, old Puma sneakers and I have a torn bag on my back. People could easily be sitting around watching me and tut-tutting at the poor *gringo* who is down on his luck. I see a bald man wearing a pink polo shirt and blue paisley shorts look me up and down because of my slovenliness. He grabs his Gucci man bag and takes a seat at the end of the bench. While juggling his load he promptly overbalances his Big Mac and coke over his lap. I suppress a smile and watch him join the ranks of the judged as he scoops special sauce from his flies.

I continue along past the *cambios* and bag shops to the escalators. I walk around the corners of the far edges, which look out to the runway and the terracotta colours of the suburb of Barajas illuminated by the streetlights.

And then I see him. I'm sitting at the café across from McDonald's now to pass the time. I notice a slim man wearing jeans and a t-shirt with a backpack on his back. He sits at a table that is yet to be cleared. After looking around for a moment he rattles the drinks on the table until he finds one that is a mostly full. He grabs it and walks straight out, flinging the lid and the straw into the bin before taking a big gulp and disappearing in the direction of the Iberia check-in desks.

It is too strange, my snooping around the airport looking people up and down, much like the pink shirted man did to me. All I want is to have a conversation with someone. It is as if I am in an urban zoo where all the exhibits look the same, which essentially they do, and I have to somehow see beyond this camouflage.

The answer is time. I talk to a green shirted *guardia civil* guard and he tells me that many people live here, "Wait a while and go up to the second floor. There's maybe forty people every night during summer who sleep there," he says.

"Is it legal?" I ask, wondering whether it is the same as Sydney Airport where they shut the doors and treat loafers and people down on their luck like criminals.

He shrugs: "It's a public space. If they don't make any problems, it is a 24-hour airport, so it never closes. What can you do?"

I slow down in order to see the movement of the airport better. A man is sitting in the shadows of a closed café sleeping in relative comfort. Soon after, I see an older man with a beard and a blue plastic bag heading for the toilets. He is wearing a suit jacket, though his missing socks don't seem like a hipster statement. I see him later come out of another exit and walk for the far corner of the terminal. I then notice another man in tracksuit trousers pushing a trolley with two blue Ikea bags full of possessions. It is now that I appreciate the differences between the people here. The travellers are either sitting and their thoughts are far-off, of home or the next stop or they have a purposeful stride moving through this place. The other people I've begun to notice look weary and familiar with the terminal. They look around furtively in order to remain camouflaged. The key for them is to blend in, carry a bag or a trolley, wear clothes that make them look like they're travelling, or they could afford a ticket. With my vision altered, straight away I notice a skinny, bearded man peeling the segments of a mandarin and popping them in his mouth. He carries a laptop bag and wears glasses. He doesn't have the walk of a traveller, and the next moment he's searching for fries in a discarded McDonald's bag.

Out behind the *cambio* exchange booths I stumble upon a man reclining on a green sleeping bag with earphones in and his hands resting on his chest. I'm not prepared and I don't know what to say.

"My name is Ben. I'm Australian. Can we have a chat, sir?" is all I muster as an awkward introduction.

He props himself up and smiles.

"I'm tired. Not tonight if that's ok?" he replies.

"Of course. What's your name?"

"Pablo. See you later," he says with a smile before plugging back in.

Later I notice the meandering gait and patience in a man with black hair and a 'Rock'n Roll' t-shirt. I approach him and ask if I might talk to him.

"Do I look like I live here?" he asks with half a smile on his face.

"Ahhh. Ummm." I don't know how to respond.

"I'm tired tonight. Maybe tomorrow," he says with another smile before walking off to another corner.

Over by the phone booths I see a slight Asian man unpacking a suitcase. He is rolling up his belt and taking off his socks. He looks like a traveller for a moment, though his familiarity with the nightly routine reveals his residency. He rolls out a sleeping bag. It is strange. It is a public space, though I feel like I'm standing at his bedroom door watching him prepare for the night. He takes off his glasses and I ask in my awkward way if I can have a chat. He looks at me for a moment, as if indeed he has just noticed someone at his bedroom door. He responds, "No, gracias," with a half smile. I retreat quickly and leave him to his imaginary privacy.

Later I meet Sefa, a Bulgarian electrician who has lived at the airport for the past two years. He has sad, drooping eyes and a face tanned from the sun. He's happy for me to sit with him as we watch the planes outside.

"There are many who've been here longer than two years," he tells me. "While there is no work this is the only place I can afford."

He has a bag of food with him; I peer in and see it is mostly pilfered from bins. He spends the day in Madrid looking for food and money and then buses back here in the evenings.

"I was an electrician in Bulgaria," he says. "I came here for work fourteen years ago and I got by doing constructions. The work stopped two years ago."

"With the crisis?" I ask.

"One of them," he answers without a smile.

Now Sefa spends his evenings looking for money in the phone boxes and the vending machines, "People are always rushing here. They leave money behind and don't think of it."

He has one luxury every day and he produces a green can of beer from his bag: "twenty-five cents," Sefa says as he cracks it open and takes a sip: "It was hot today, no?"

I nod and he tells me that it's fine living here. He has friends and they have a *jefe*, a former police officer named Geraldo who has emphysema and is the unofficial boss of T4.

"We pay him in cigarettes to make sure everything is fine."

I see a bed roll in the corner and I ask if it's his.

"No, that's someone else's."

He pats his pink Reebok bag,

"My bed is in here."

I offer to buy him another beer as he drains the last from his can, though he says he's fine and it's time to get some rest.

"Thank you for your time," I say as I leave Sefa. He smiles and says, "You're most welcome," happy for the chat and the brief connection as I disappear around the corner.

Terminal 4 (Panhard/Wikimedia Commons)

The next resident I meet is Rafael. He is older than many of the people I see living here and has a long grey ponytail. He has the same slow walk as the others and after a few moments where he is suspicious of my motives, he changes from Spanish to perfect English.

"So you want to know what it's like to live at the airport?"

I nod, hoping not to offend. He seems happy to talk to someone in English and he props himself up on a bench.

"My wife and I have been living here for four and a half months," he says.

He is Venezuelan, though he has spent many years in Madrid and he went to university at McGill in Canada where he became a chemical engineer. "I met many Australians when I was at Uni. I liked them. They seemed worldly. Not like the Americans, who still think it all revolves around them."

I ask him what it's like here.

"It's ok. We have some friends in the city. We don't tell them we live here. We just say that we're staying with a relative and leave it at that."

He explains that during the day they try and be as normal as possible, "We go to museums and galleries when they have free entry, like the Prado just before closing. I spend most days looking for food for us. There are a few shelters and churches we can go to for this."

Rafael tells me that he and his wife have been in Madrid for sixteen years, though he doesn't say what led them to T4. He tells me that three times a week health workers come out to check on them and to recruit them as well.

"Recruit?" I ask.

"For the shelters in the city," he says.

"Why don't you go?" I ask.

"They're more dangerous than here. You get stuff stolen all the time, you have to share with people who snore, and because my wife and I would be separated anyway, we're much better coming here."

Rafael seems in no rush to break off our conversation. We move to the side of one of the long corridors to chat more comfortably. He tells me that at the beginning living at the airport seems nice, "There's hot water, lots of paper. Some people wash their clothes here. You see the planes coming and going and it's exciting at the start, though after a while when you see all the people leaving, and you can't, it gets depressing."

I ask how they survive the day-to-day here.

"I have a pension, because I'm 66, so I pay €12 a month for a travel pass. I took ten buses and three trains today."

He also says that each day they go and have showers in the city, "It's fifty cents a shower, though I often pay double for a good soak."

They then wash their clothes at a launderette and take a bus back out here.

Rafael tells me there are about forty residents here and many survive from drug deals or stealing from other residents and travellers. Some of them, "should be in institutions, for crazy people," he says as he twirls his index finger around the outside of his head.

"There is one lady from Guyana. She's crazy, and dangerous. She tells some people she has AIDS and cuts herself and threatens to infect them. She has a warrant out for her arrest, though what can you do? If I hit her I'd go to jail, and them my wife would be alone."

He says she broke someone's arm the other week and she steals from residents all the time.

"You learn how to survive here. It's the only way."

The police here often do raids and wake them up in the middle of the night to check papers. "It's good though, it means most of the criminals are arrested."

Rafael also says that because of the terror attacks in Europe recently they're on high alert, so it'll probably happen tonight.

Just as Sefa confirmed, Rafael also tells me that Geraldo looks after them all, as an unofficial sheriff of the people who live in T4. We wander towards check-in counter 758, near where Rafael and his wife will sleep tonight and we see Geraldo preparing for the night. He smells of tobacco and when Rafael introduces me, he is short with his reply, though he said he'd be happy to chat in the café tomorrow maybe.

"He's grumpy, but he's our guardian angel. He has a relationship with the police here so we're all mostly ok," he says.

I ask if this will be a permanent thing and he shrugs and laughs a little: "Who knows? Our family is expecting an inheritance one of these days, though like all families when it comes to money, there will be fights, so I don't know."

Rafael is going off to meet his wife, so he shakes my hand and we wish each other well. It is a little strange; seeing as only fifty metres away there are people doing exactly the same thing before they depart on planes and fly away from here, rather than curling up in a corner until the sun comes up and the challenges begin again tomorrow.

I wander off, as I want to get an official perspective on this microcosm. At the police desk I ask the lady if I can ask her a few questions. She nods and says, "Of course."

But when I start asking questions about the homeless she stonewalls me like a politician.

"So does anything ever happen with the homeless here?"

"Not generally."

"How many would you say are here?"

"Oh, I couldn't say?"

"Thirty, forty?"

"I couldn't say."

"Or won't?" I ask.

She shrugs; it's the same. I thank her for her time and try the same line with the 24-hour information desk.

"Do you have much interaction with the homeless people here?" I ask.

"There aren't any homeless here," she responds.

My brow crinkles at the lie.

"There are some people on Ryanair and easyJet who sleep here because they don't want to pay for a hotel."

"What about all the people sleeping over there? They're not flying anywhere tomorrow," I respond, pointing to the people stretched out in the near corner.

"I really couldn't say. Maybe in Terminal 2 there are some?"

She's lying and she knows I know, but she can't say. I have a feeling that ignorance might be the official line here.

"The airport allows the people sleeping there to remain anonymous," Darío Pérez, head of Samur Social, the division of Spain's emergency health services that provides care for homeless people and the vulnerable, told *El País*, though it seems the officials are quite happy for them to be anonymous as well.

I decide that it's time I left the people here to their rest, though as I'm heading for departures a skinny Nigerian man approaches me. He's crying and he blubbers, "Please help me."

I wonder if he has recently got off a plane or if this is his ruse and he lives here too. Christopher tells me that Caritas flew him here from Abuja in Nigeria. He has no cash and he has to get to Barcelona—if I can spare anything. Being sceptical is a luxury of the haves rather than the have nots, though I still ask him how they could fly him all the way here and not leave him with even enough for a bus fare.

"It's complicated," he says through the tears.

Even if it isn't, I'm sure his position is a desperate one so I give him a few euros before he continues crying and approaches another tourist. I hear "It's complicated!" as he wails and in the distance I see a woman enter the terminal. She is bald and her teeth are bared revealing red gums. Her swollen ankles are covered in bandages and she leers at a group of tourists who recoil as she kicks a five-cent coin at them. This is the lady from Guyana Rafael warned me about. I decide to take his advice and I catch the lift down to the Metro where I board the next train into the city.

12am: The Ritz

Whoever thinks of going to bed before twelve o'clock is a scoundrel.
Samuel Johnson

The seconds seem to build momentum on my watch as if it's pushing towards New Year: 55, 56, 57, 58, 59 and then it's 12am. It feels significant for a moment though it is only a regular Saturday. It is a new day, yet the night is the same. As one second pushes Madrid from pm to am on the clock at Atocha I decide to retrace my first steps up along the Paseo del Prado in the first moments of the morning. I do this partly because I also don't want to be lost again so soon. Thin clouds brush past the moon, which is now high in the night sky. People appear less frequently than they did a few hours ago once I exit out onto the streets from the station.

The Ritz (Luis García/Wikimedia Commons)

There is space on the *paseo* and there are pockets of silence as I walk. The energy of earlier in the night has settled somewhat; the city is pensive as it ticks from one day and into the next as 12:01 and Saturday begins.

I can hear the water in the fountains slushing onto the stones, the wail of an ambulance in the distance and the scuffing of footsteps behind me as I walk. The Botanic Garden is closed, as are most of the businesses across the road. Up ahead are the sounds of music and a crowd chattering. Some new-age flamenco is playing softly from a garden and it draws me to the edge of the Hotel Ritz like a window shopper. Blue fairy lights are strung up around the outdoor restaurant. I see the doorman still standing regally in his hat and coat at the entrance to the hotel, waiting to open the door for returning guests, despite the hour, so I decide to enter as well.

The Ritz is old-school opulence: thick, hand-made carpets, cabinets of caviar and winding staircases a hundred years old. I want to understand the life that exists here at night beyond the veneer presented by the rich and privileged guests.

Teresa Dorn, a former journalist from the Canary Islands who now works in the hotel, is my contact. She opens the doors that allow me to see the night-time activities in the Ritz. Guests who look like characters from the Steve Martin and Michael Caine film *Dirty Rotten Scoundrels* walk through the corridors, complete with slicked hair, unnaturally white teeth and loafers. A man who fits this description comes and sits on the seat next to me, crossing his legs to reveal sockless slip-ons. He looks at the staircase, and then to his watch: "Women hey!" he says in a Texan drawl by way of an icebreaker while shaking his head. There is soft lounge music, the air is lightly perfumed with jasmine and everything feels serene and stress-free. I smile at the man; it's my Anglo politeness kicking in, when I'd rather tell him to do something else. My wife is Argentinian, cut from the same cloth as the *Madrileños* and she is spontaneous and late for everything. At first I thought it was rude and disrespectful of her and I was often embarrassed, though it has taken me years to realize that respect means much more than showing up on time to something you don't even want to go to. Even if we're forty minutes late to a friend's dinner, she'll talk and actually listen to people, rather than nodding through pleasantries until it is a polite time to leave. Being late and genuine seems much more meaningful to me, though it's something I've had to learn. With that I get up and leave Mr. Smug to his watch. I'm not interested in these people or the view from above. I want another perspective, so I head for a side door next to the lift.

I start at the bottom, literally. From the opulent lobby full of chandeliers, champagne and lounge music I descend below the hotel.

As soon as I open the door at the base of the stairs the energy is different. A plate smashes as it clatters under the stainless steel benches of the kitchen, a man yells as blue flames shoot from his sizzling pan and I'm bumped out of the way by a worker in white, who is chattering on a phone about candlesticks and walking towards a swinging door. While everyone from Salvador Dalí to Tina Turner might have stayed in the luxurious surrounds of the Ritz, the people who make it function at night, so it can run smoothly during the day, live below, like subterranean beings subject to a different rhythm to those who enjoy the benefits of their labour above. They work when it is dark and sleep during the day.

I watch a chef sear scallops with a press of his metal spatula and another squirt thick black squid ink onto a bowl of pasta. All the workers have their heads down in concentration. Many of them seem separate from the noise and the commotion around them so absorbed are they by the pattern they are creating while plating up or the curl of the fennel on the edge of a salad.

The chaos in the kitchen does not seem like it will abate soon, so I edge towards a quieter corner, where two pastry chefs are studiously working to produce 120 tartlets for tomorrow morning's service. Ramón González has worked here since 1990 and he is one of the six pastry chefs at the Ritz. Ramón and Karim El Mahsouri are slowly placing berries on top of pastry shells, each no bigger than the face of a watch, with the sort of caution I would expect from a surgeon manoeuvring through open-heart surgery. The chefs' hands are sturdy as if used to slicing a ventricle rather than placing a berry on a bed of custard. Karim tells me he loves this city, and he doesn't mind working at night: "Everyone is happy here, food is good and it's cheap enough to live well," he says. It is cool and quiet in his little corner; he shakes ever so slightly as the raspberry from his fingertips drops into place.

I continue through the bustling and noisy corridors. Over by the enormous silver dishwashers, a man who is rinsing stainless steel food tubs with a hose that looks designed to put out house fires glances up at me. He cuts the hose and stops for a chat while he puts another machine into action to sear the grime off the silver platters.

Moses, the dishwasher, arrived in Madrid from Kenya seven years ago. His brother was studying here and he came over as a tourist to visit him. He liked the opportunities and the rhythm of the city compared to his home. Moses has been here ever since and is now married with a young daughter.

"I went back to Kenya last year, though because I'm a temp worker I lost my job. They called me back three months ago because they needed someone dependable to fill in, and I didn't have anything else." He is aware of the dire employment situation in Madrid. "I'm happy because I have a job, but everything is so fragile, I'm a migrant, I'm black, there is huge unemployment here, so I can't push too hard." Moses also thinks these are all reasons why he hasn't progressed as he might have hoped in the hospitality industry. He dips the silver spoons and candlesticks into a basin filled with a caustic smelling green chemical while we chat.

"There are eighty kilogrammes of ball bearings inside the machine that clean off all the grit," he says. Glasses smash behind us and there is more shouting from the kitchen, though Moses is happy for the break in his night-time monotony of washing others' dishes.

Vintage luxury at the Ritz (Freesun News)

The Presidential Suite in Madrid's Ritz costs €11,000 per night. Moses earns a touch more than this in an entire year, though he says it gives his family enough to survive.

The Ritz Madrid was built at the behest of King Alfonso XIII. Around the start of the twentieth century, Madrid was beginning to rival other European capitals, Paris and London, with its culture and history, coupled with blue skies and finer weather than either. But it lacked a top quality hotel. Alfonso enlisted Carlos Ritz to build the hotel he wanted for his city in 1908. Six million pesetas (the currency of the time) and two years later, it opened on 3 October 1910. English silver cutlery was brought in, two kilometres of carpets were handmade and four or five shared bathrooms per floor were installed, relative luxury at the time, for the soon to be paying guests.

The Ritz was eventually joined in Madrid by other luxury hotels such as the nearby Palace, though it continually grew in size and reputation, housing actors, writers, performers and nobility. During World War I, Spain remained neutral, though many dignitaries fled to Madrid and holed up at the Ritz for sanctuary. One of the most infamous guests was the bejewelled Dutch ballet dancer Mata Hari. She was a double agent, working with the French and secretly passing on information to the Germans for profit. She would seduce the French over tea at the Ritz, though they didn't trust the dancer from Leeuwarden and she was later exposed as a spy and executed in Paris by firing squad in 1917 for her treason that began in Madrid's most renowned hotel.

Despite avoiding World War I, conflict eventually found its way to the Ritz. Leftist soldiers barricaded themselves inside the hotel during the worst of the fighting with Franco's forces during the civil war, and later it was used as a military hospital where the rooms became wards and the salons were transformed into operating theatres. Buenaventura Durruti, the charismatic leftist leader, who had been a major reason for the enduring solidarity and resistance among *Madrileños* and for the delay of Franco's capture of the city, was shot on 20 November 1936, accidentally as it happened, as the machine gun of a companion caught in a door handle and fired a round into his chest. It was on the operating tables of the Ritz that doctors tried, in vain, to save his life.

I think of this, nearly eighty years later, in the same hotel, as I watch the men and women in white rushing in the noise, flames and heat all around amidst the smell of cooking meat from the grill. There is a saying at the Ritz, that "the show must go on" and this has always been the case at the hotel. During the civil war when doctors and nurses worked through the night, there were still paying guests in other wings, and in 1939 at the close of the conflict, the hotel had crockery, cutlery, uniforms and furniture brought in "at the head of a fleet of trucks" so as to resume business as usual as soon as possible; in war, dictatorship or, like now, at night, in its modern setting it kept its doors open. Capitalism trumps all in the end, it seems.

I watch chefs as they fillet fish and whip sauces into shape. Dinner service is available until 1am here, not including room service, which is 24-hour, so the pressure won't be relieved for a while. I head back up the stairs to "walk the hotel", first with room service manager Eva, who makes sure that slippers are positioned correctly and that the corners of every bed are turned down. She says that they even have a special shift at night for cleaning the white sofas of the Presidential Suite. As we enter the long wood-panelled room I can see that it is ornate, though to me it seems like just a room in which to sleep and have a shower. Despite its cost, it has a 60 per cent occupancy throughout the year, and most recently Salma Hayek and her brood stayed in the suite.

Out in the quiet corridor I meet Emma, the duty manager of the Ritz, from Chile. At night she walks every corridor, stairway and alcove in the hotel to make sure that it is all functioning smoothly; she checks the unseen machine the guests are blind to and tinkers where necessary to keep it purring. Emma invites me to join her on her walk from the lobby up to the very top of the hotel to see it at night.

It is quiet on the roof of the Ritz. We walk out on the slim, metal grates in the open air to a ledge. From here we can see down the Paseo del Prado and across the city. The old streets are lit with an orange glow and beside them the suburbs stretch out to the horizon. Night time and darkness are different things in modern cities; the pockets of real darkness are much scarcer than you would imagine. Taxi drivers mill below waiting for fares, street cleaners are out with their high-tech trucks and hoses; bars and restaurants keep their doors open in the hope of one more glass of wine or whisky from a patron; work never stops in the city.

In the Middle Ages many forms of work were deemed illegal at night, due to religious objection or the fear of fire (from a forge) or inferior workmanship; as early as the twelfth century English and French guilds prevented workers such as gold and silversmiths from working at night to maintain the quality and reputation of their work. One of the commodities to push early modern Europe towards a 24-hour working day was beer. In Sweden and the Netherlands beer production was so important that breweries were permitted to operate through the night, fermenting their batches for the next day. Later, perishables such as calves' blood and shellfish would be hawked in the streets of seaside Italy, as they would not last through the next day—and so the night-time economy was born. Later, rag pickers, weavers, tailors, shoemakers, fishermen, candlewick makers, glassmakers, night men who emptied chamber pots and privies and salt boilers would all join the industrial drive to work at night as technology allowed and demand required. For a long time, a civilization's worst tasks were reserved for the cover of night. As A. Roger Ekirch notes, "during epidemics, municipal officials waited for darkness to dispose of their dead." It was thought that the quiet and vacant streets of the night would minimize the spread of infections and general panic. In London during the plague of 1665, which killed 56,000 people, "dead-carts" were wheeled out at night for families to bring out their deceased. Whether using moonlight to chop wood, or candles to bake bread, the night has now been a time to be awake and working for centuries. The Spanish saying "The sun set, the workman freed" has not applied in Europe, or Madrid, for a long time.

The noises of the city are distant from our high perch above the hotel and lights twinkle all across this expanse of six million people. Emma smiles and tells me that her time inspecting the exits on the roof is the highlight of her night.

"I can breathe out here," she says with a smile. We pause for a minute, maybe two and just watch the city in silence as it blinks and twitches in flashes of yellow, red, white and orange against the black sky.

We open the fire door again and descend back inside the Ritz, Emma peeps along halls and nods to maids as we walk. She tells me the stories of the people here as we check fire exits and stairwells, "One guest we have comes and goes from the hotel a few times a year, though he always leaves his car here in Madrid. Every week we have to drive it around the block so it doesn't seize up and so it's ready for him whenever he comes back," she says. Another guest always rents a room for himself to sleep in, and another to smoke in. Other guests want the same room that they've been staying in for forty years. "It's not always possible," she says as we walk down the quiet corridors passing a room service attendant as he pushes a trolley along the thick carpet.

"So sometimes we change the furniture and the fittings in a room so it resembles the one they are used to," she says. "People come here for its legend," she adds. Back down on ground level Emma shows me the secret door that leads across to the Museo del Prado from the back entrance of the Felipe IV function room.

"For notable people we'll often take them out in secret at night and open the museum so they can experience it in peace," she tells me. She also says that with a place such as this, the guests' expectations that the staff will go beyond their call of duty is quite normal: "All the time guests will bring their dogs, and then expect us to walk them while they're here." Emma and I wind through the staff dining room to the underground corridors which are lit with fluorescent lights and smell of bleach. We arrive back up at the edge of the garden restaurant where I first noticed the Ritz. People still sit and drink cocktails and eat *tapas* as if it is 8pm in any other city.

Emma leaves me at the front desk where the concierge, David Rodríguez, has just returned from a motorbike trip across the city to secure some last minute tickets for a guest. The concierge workers are legendary at the Ritz for being able to get anything at any time for their guests, whether it is a date for the evening or esoteric animal advice.

David tells me: "A little while ago a Brazilian guest bought an exotic parrot from a market in the city, and they wanted to know how they could get it back to Brazil. We had to organize insurance and shipping, but eventually the parrot made it home."

The concierge at the Ritz, where reputation and going beyond the call of duty are expected, performs miracles on a nightly basis. David continues talking as we stand behind his little desk in the corner. "One American guest was with his son, who was a football fan. He wanted a trainer for his son while they were here, so I got a coach from Atlético Madrid to play football with him."

I'm sure a whole book could be filled with the confessions of a concierge, though as David says, "There are many stories I can't tell you," referring to the implicit trust the guests place in the concierge to get them everything and anything they can't procure themselves.

"Once we had a Saudi prince stay with us, and he wanted to take a train to Seville," Jesus Toledo, the other concierge on night duty, tells me.

"Ok…" I say, uncertainly.

"He's one of the twenty richest people on earth. He wanted to go to Seville by train, but he wanted the whole train to himself. And he wanted to leave first thing the next morning."

David laughs as he remembers the story.

"We had to run around ringing the managers of the train company in the middle of the night, but we did it and he travelled the two and a half hours to Seville the next morning in his very own train," says Jesus.

"And it only cost him €50,000!" adds David.

From the concierge I go to the Krug Bar, a quiet and classy cocktail corner with red leather seats and black and white pictures on the walls of the notable guests who have pulled up a stool here over the years. I'm the only patron.

"It's still early," the barman, Jonathan, tells me.

He's new; this is his second day on the job, so he makes me a Dalí-tini to practise while we sit. He tells me the story of Salvador Dalí in the hotel and how he came to have a cocktail named after him. Dalí came to the Ritz for a haircut in 1926 and took a detour to the bar. He ordered a cocktail and inadvertently cut his finger on the rim of the glass. He dipped the blood into his drink and laced it with a maraschino cherry in one smooth motion, and the surrealist twist on the Martini was born.

Another man famous for his cocktails at the Ritz was Perico Chicote; he started at the hotel in 1916 as a seventeen-year-old. He had a passion for collecting rare and interesting alcohol, and when the Ambassador of Brazil gave him a bottle of Paraty spirits, it began a collection which would be known in Madrid as the "museum of drinks"; he had 18,000 liquor bottles in all, including vodka from Russian tsars and cognac that had been sipped by Napoleon. Eventually Chicote opened the Museo Chicote on Gran Vía and for a long time it was said to have the most extensive cocktail list in the world.

In the roaring 1920s, young artists Dalí, García Lorca and the filmmaker Luis Buñuel all had a connection to the hotel. They had met at the Students' Residence or "Resi", a free-thinking educational experiment developed to support liberal study and a broad cultural perspective for its students in the suburb of Salamanca, to the north-west of Madrid.

These three young students, who would all become revolutionaries and legends in their fields, frequented the jazz club on the ground floor of the Ritz, slamming back double vodkas as the Jackson Brothers played into the night. As Elizabeth Nash notes, much of Dalí's, Lorca's and Buñuel's money at the time went on these night-time extravaganzas; nocturnal strolling was also one of their favourite pastimes. Dalí's 1922 surrealist watercolour *Night-Walking Dreams* was inspired by their after-dark adventures in Madrid, where they would do everything from walking the streets dressed as priests to frequently visiting the brothels of the city. I drain the last of my tart, vodka-tasting cocktail and walk to one of the few areas that is busier at night here in the hotel.

In reception I meet Julia. She is blonde with red-rimmed glasses and a British accent, "I'm Romanian," she tells me to counter my assumption. I'm shown the job of the night receptionist, who is basically in charge of the whole hotel until the sun comes up once the night manager leaves. She is one of the many foreign workers at the Ritz, where the majority are non-Spanish and come from all over the world. At night she processes all payments, schedules the wake-up calls and the taxis for tomorrow, and is the on-call person for the rest of the skeleton staff above ground.

"I've got to organize an early morning helicopter pickup for one of our guests too," she adds.

"Want to see something?" Julia asks me as I walk behind the counter.

I nod and she reveals the secret button under the counter.

"It's my panic button. I have a code word. If I press the button the police will call and if I say anything else other than the code word they'll be here in minutes," she says.

"So if I say 'Hi, yes, everything's fine,' then they'll bring tactical police."

"And have you pressed it?" I ask.

"Yes, I bumped it once for real. And another time there was a fire in the kitchen and we had to evacuate the building," She says with a half smile. Julia thumps a pile of invoices on the counter and, considering I'm not a work experience student, I decide to leave her to the hours of processing. I walk to the front door, this time to exit the Ritz. As I leave I chat to the doorman who has a big grin and frosty blue eyes. Juan García has worked here for more than twenty years, "My job is to smile," he tells me. He grew up only 300 metres from the Ritz and he has lived in this city, and worked at the Ritz, his entire life. His shift is coming to an end.

He has opened the door all night and as the stream of guests thins, he finishes until tomorrow.

I have seen the richest of the rich and the one per cent that the Ocupa movement is so indignant about. Despite the stories and the history of the Ritz, luxury and wealth look largely similar all over the world. I want to experience something of the other side of the city to get some perspective, so I decide to head south.

1am: Outer *barrio* walking

Come and see the blood in the streets
Come and see
The blood in the streets
Come and see the blood
In the streets.
Pablo Neruda, "I'm Explaining A Few Things", 1937

Teresa skewers another pig's ear from the plate and follows it with a mouthful of mashed and congealed blood sausage.

"This place is an institution," she says of the Bar La Morcilla. It is packed with boisterous locals who all stand on the grubby linoleum littered with chunks of sausage and dirty napkins. "Hola Manuel!" Teresa yells across the floor to the bartender. I get the impression that everyone knows everyone here, except for me. We drain our *cañas* and begin an exploration of Villaverde, the poor suburb on the southern periphery of Madrid which I have been told is too dangerous for me to enter alone.

This is a suburb which was once full of farms and had a village atmosphere; it now predominantly comprises grey apartment buildings and concrete play areas broken up by large tracts of *campo* where the long grass and eroded gullies hide its secrets. My guides in Villaverde are Teresa and Isabel, two middle-aged ladies in floral dresses who suck from their hand rolled cigarettes as we walk. Despite appearances, these two women have more *calle* in them, as a sense of the streets is called here, than most people in the city. Many of Villaverde's stories come from the scars it bears from the post-Franco years, though Teresa reminds me that this *barrio* was an important location during the civil war in the 1930s that brought General Franco to power.

Spain in the 1930s was a tumultuous place as factions from the Falangist and nationalist right and the socialist and republican left fought for Madrid's streets and political control of Spain. In February 1936 the left-wing Frente Popular coalition of socialists and communists was elected to government, and the forces of the right, including large parts of the nation's military, went into revolt, unwilling to abide a socialist Spain. On 17 July 1936 a group of officers from the Spanish military's high command declared a *coup d état* to overthrow the government. The uprising began in the Spanish territories of North Africa, namely Melilla and Ceuta in Morocco, with forces controlled by General Francisco Franco, who had quelled leftist movements earlier in the decade.

Franco was the son of a naval postmaster and joined Toledo's infantry academy as a fifteen-year-old. He later spent ten years in Africa fighting a colonial war and it was there that he developed a reputation as a brave and ruthless military leader. Franco was seen by many as a national hero because of his role in Africa and as the *coup* gained momentum, Spain's youngest general manoeuvred his way to the top of the nationalist forces. In the summer of 1936 Franco's army stormed towards the capital to wrest power from the anarchy of the "godless red hordes". The "Africa Army", as it was known, ploughed through resistance in the Spanish countryside with relative ease. Franco was named *generalisimo* and the army fanned out for a three-pronged attack on Madrid by October. Franco assumed that the fall of Madrid would be straightforward as the nationalists had 40,000 troops descending on the capital. The fighters for the republican left were said to be a passionate, but disorganized and inexperienced force.

Republican troops on the march in Madrid, September 1936 (Mikhail Koltsov/Wikimedia Commons)

Franco's first objective, to take the Republic by a *coup*, failed as seven of Spain's nine biggest cities remained loyal to the elected Frente Popular government. From this setback Franco changed approach and, with the help of 70,000 troops sent by Mussolini's Italy and the Condor Legion from Hitler's Germany, settled in for the long fight. Franco's army burst through the left's defences and by 23 October, with the help of the Italian air force and the Luftwaffe (the early Nazi air squadrons), began bombing Madrid. Personnel from the Soviet Union, Mexico and 6,000 volunteer fighters forming the International Brigades assisted the republican left. Despite the ferocity of the attack they held out for months as the bravery of the normal citizens kept the city intact.

In the Plaza de Atocha there was a placard that read: "In Badajoz the Fascists shot 2,000. If Madrid falls they will shoot half the city." This referred to the massacre in the provincial town in Extremadura, where the people tried in vain to resist the invasion. The nationalists rounded up the remaining republican fighters, said to be around 2,000, and herded them into the local bullring, where they were all executed by machine gun fire under the orders of General Yagüe.

Despite the atrocities which occurred in Badajoz, news of the events strengthened the resolve of Madrid's citizens not to give up their city without a fight, as they knew what might happen if they lost. Women and children helped erect barricades from rocks and timber. Previously disengaged *Madrileños* dug trenches in the streets and prepared their city for fighting that would pass through every alley and doorway of Madrid before it was done.

The battle moved up from the south-west through Villaverde and the suburbs towards the open parkland of Casa de Campo in the city. In Villaverde itself there were vicious street-by-street battles, soldiers slashing with bayonets, grenades being lobbed along the thoroughfares and fighting so chaotic that often men did not know who was in front or behind as they smashed through kitchen windows, across family patios and out into the streets again to defend their territory. There were delays, reversals and important victories for the republicans. Franco's army did not seem as invincible as it was once thought. The city still held out and the battle continued. Many of the observing journalists and foreign soldiers noted the people's resolve during the conflict and their ability to get on with life despite the anarchy around them. Antony Beevor cites the reaction of an

English bombardier watching a *Madrileño* standing in the middle of the street during an offensive and "nonchalantly picking his teeth with a match" as bombs exploded in the street around him. The outsiders, particularly republican sympathizers, saw the bravery of the citizens as poetic; they refused to give up their lives and cower during the fighting.

When the nationalists crossed the River Manzanares in Madrid, the first city street fighting began, of all places on the university campus overlooking the Casa de Campo. At this stage the nationalists were only a few hundred metres from entering the city itself. They fought through the laboratories and classrooms; the republicans constructed barricades from volumes of the *Encyclopaedia Britannica* and they held off the attack again.

The streets were virtually impassable now and the government ferried paintings and valuables out of the conflict zones through the unused tunnels of the Metro. More than half a million *Madrileños* left the city during the conflict, and in 1937 the war became a winter stalemate; roaming packs of dogs developed a taste for human flesh on the rubble-strewn streets and each side positioned snipers in the city in hope of winning a war of attrition. Franco's nationalists aimed shells into all the most populated parts of the city, resulting in more than 4,000 dead and wounded. The eventual downfall of Madrid seemed just as inevitable as the bull's death in the *corrida*.

But a quick death did not come. The city was encircled and the nationalists could not dislodge the grip of the republican fighters, so Franco moved to other battles and conquests in Spain until 1939, when the starving, orphaned city finally waved the white flag in defeat. On 1 April Franco announced that the war was finally over. In the wake of the battle more than 250,000 Spaniards went into exile permanently and 33,000 children were sent to the Soviet Union, the United Kingdom and Mexico among other places by their republican parents.

Franco went on to rule as one of the modern world's most ruthless dictators. Some estimates put the deaths during and after the war as high as 200,000, and Franco was brutal in his reprisals after the conflict. While taking his morning coffee he would mark a notepad full of prisoners' names with either an "E" for execute or a "C" to commute the sentence, and he would make specific examples of some with an extra instruction to garrotte them in public and to ensure press coverage. Madrid became a cold and suspicious place, much like Nazi Berlin, and the streets were full of spies and informants.

In a reflection on the importance of the night in Madrid, Franco revived the *serenos*, the night watchmen, who were first introduced to the dark streets of Madrid during Carlos IV's reign in 1797. They would light the street lamps, call out the weather and let late night arrivals into their homes. In their reincarnation, however, their more useful function as they walked the streets from 10pm until 7am was to inform Franco of any suspicious activity by *Madrileños* who were hoping for the cover of darkness. These *serenos* were not dismissed from the city until 1977 and they numbered 1,300 at the end of his rule.

☾

There are no longer *serenos* on the streets of Villaverde and we walk the quiet *avenidas* alone as Teresa and Isabel tell me the stories of their suburb after dark. From the packed bar we walk up past the Metro station, which is still busy at this time of the early morning. Many people are descending the stairs to take a train into the city to begin their night. Down the hill we see prostitutes parading along the dark streets and car windows slowly rolling down to negotiate fees with the women.

"All the *prostitutas* used to be in the Casa de Campo," Teresa says, referring to the family-oriented parkland in the centre of the city that was also one of the key battlegrounds of the civil war. "The government cleaned up the park and they all ended up here outside the Metro. They still work for the Russian mafia though," Isabel adds.

We walk down Calle Escribanos, past shoe shops and an infants' school that Teresa started for the community.

There are groups of men and boys sitting on the corners, some leaning on their motorbikes, others smoking cigarettes in the dark. It's mostly safe here now; we walk along to the *plaza*. It is late, but families still sit on the benches under the streetlights talking and playing cards. Children ride rusty bikes and play with dolls in the gardens behind their parents. There is a sense of simple happiness here in the dark, though much of this is enforced idling.

"Most of these people don't have jobs," Teresa says. "They don't have anything to get up for tomorrow, so they enjoy the nights together.

Unemployment is worse than 25 per cent in Villaverde," she adds. We see men in singlets laughing and playing *chinchón* (a local card game). As one man slaps down a stack of worn cards, another scoops up his collection of coins. Gambling is a central part of enjoyment in Madrid, from the numerous bingo clubs in the city, through to impromptu card games for beer money on the night corners.

This love of gambling, like many activities in Madrid's night time, has its roots in the post-Franco era. Aside from the killing and torture of political and ideological opponents, Franco's Spain was a repressed country, where sex outside of marriage, gambling, education, regional languages in the Basque and Catalan regions, media freedom and labour unions were all stifled under the *generalisimo*'s complete control until his death, while still ruling, in 1975.

In the aftermath of Franco's death, the Spanish became "a bit like the archetypal ex-convent schoolgirl, recklessly experimenting with everything previously forbidden," according to John Hooper. While during the dictatorship people were said to have a "culture of evasion", escaping into romantic films, plays, football and lotteries, once the general died this was replaced with the "culture of addiction". This era of freedom and experimentation took many forms, including prostitution; immediately after the fall of Franco's regime it was said that one in twenty-five women were "on the game" and earned money from prostitution in order to survive. This, in a strange way, intersects with another statistic, that one in four Spanish men has had had a *turno* with a prostitute in their lives—the highest proportion in Europe. Apart from sex, commercial or not, there was also an enormous influx of drugs into Spain through the smuggling routes in the south from Africa and through Galicia in the north. It is not known why, considering the availability of hashish and cocaine from Morocco and South America respectively, but heroin became the drug of choice in post-Franco Madrid.

Strangely, creating a further incendiary development, the socialist government that came into power after Franco decided to legalize all forms of narcotics, for both public and private consumption. This move did not have the liberating effect that was hoped for. It was not unusual to see people injecting in doorways and city parks, and this was an all-consuming problem until methadone was finally offered as an alternative in 1990.

Teresa tells me that she was here in Villaverde's *plaza* in the 1970s when everything in Madrid was changing: "Junkies would be shuffling around like zombies outside our house all night." In the years after Franco's death when *la transición* began, Villaverde was at the centre of the hard drug wave that hit the city after decades of repression, largely because of its poorer demographic.

"I remember seeing a young man sitting over there one night," she says, pointing to a stone bench across from the cafés. "He was carefully heating up heroin on his little spoon and I went over to watch what he was doing."

"He wasn't hiding or being discreet?" I ask.

Teresa shakes her head: "It was new to everyone. I'd never seen heroin before. I was curious."

We walk over and sit on the same bench, where the stone is cool despite the temperature of the air. "As the drug began to bubble up on his spoon he started laughing," she says.

"Why?"

"He asked me, 'Is this what we've been fighting for all this time?' He injected right here in the *plaza*. I'm sure he's dead now," she adds as we continue walking through the Villaverde night.

The other impact that this free market on drugs had in the city was the spread of HIV/AIDS. By 1992 almost two-thirds of people with HIV in Spain were heroin addicts. In the early 1990s Spain had the highest rate of HIV in Europe and up to one-third of people in prison had contracted the disease. When the government was asked to provide clean needles for prisons, it responded with a massive distribution of bleach as an alternative. This story also cuts Isabel quite deeply, as her ex-husband and the father of her three children was a junkie in the transition era and died of AIDS in the 1990s.

We walk through to the square at the end of the path and the fountain is off for the night. A beer can and a few cigarette butts float in the still, green water. There is a giant turtle statue on the corner of the street and a bronze of a woman resting her hands on her belly. No one really has any idea what it means or why it's there. The kids seem to like using it as a jungle gym, though, Teresa says.

There are a few old junkies who have survived *la transición*. Teresa says you see them arrive around 8am and they just sit in the *plaza* and drink big cans of beer called "junkie *latas*" all day until they score. Villaverde was a wild place until recently; "even the police couldn't enter." Teresa says that the dealers would block access into the *barrio* and a night walk as we're doing now would have been unthinkable, even for locals.

Villaverde is a neighbourhood that has undergone many changes. Aside from the civil war and the drug fallout, it also wasn't so long ago that it was a quiet and tranquil spot and one of the more beautiful parts of Madrid. Teresa talks of the *arroyo*, the creek, that used to run through here and would often flood the low-lying houses when it burst its banks after a winter storm. The women are lost in their thoughts for a moment as they speak of a different time when this was a green and even bucolic place. It is grey and carcinogenic now.

"It used to be a village," says Teresa. "I remember a man used to stand on that corner," she says, pointing towards the railway crossing. "He'd sell us shellfish when I was a kid and my mother would boil them up for us in a big pot," she smiles.

We walk past the Iglesia de San Félix, a church that helps many in Villaverde during the night when they don't have anywhere to go or anyone to turn to. We walk to the edges of the suburb. There are clusters of big, brown apartment buildings on the side of the road. The *torres*, or towers, as they are called here are five apartment blocks of eight storeys each. Teresa says that homelessness was a problem here in the 1990s, so the government decided to fix the problem on the streets, at least aesthetically. They built the *torres* and rounded up all the homeless people in the *barrio*. They then proceeded to put four people in each apartment irrespective of whether they were junkies, *gitanos*, immigrants or just people down on their luck. It didn't matter; these strangers were now housemates and the problem, at least as far as the government was concerned, was solved. The tenants, for their part, were expected to play happy families because they had been provided with a roof to sleep under. It wasn't quite that simple, though, Teresa adds. The *torres* are now a magnet for people on the edges of Madrid society. Broken glass crunches under my feet and I see kids who can barely reach the pedals whizz past on scooters up and over the train lines which divide the suburb. We walk past rows of squatters living in dimly lit garages and storefronts around the edge of the apartments. Their roller doors are up and the bare rooms look like they might have been shops once, with discarded shelves and mirrors. Families live inside, and I see a portable gas burner, candles giving flickering light within the single room, an overturned trolley being used as a table and milk crates as chairs. The people inside look like any other family in Villaverde. They're out in the cool evening chatting and watching their kids, with no obvious sense of stigma borne from the fact that they're squatting and have nowhere else to go. As we pass, they smile and say "buenas", the local greeting for "good evening", and Teresa replies with familiarity.

The edges of Villaverde are still wild. Teresa says I *could* come here by myself, though it's much safer if you know someone from the neighbourhood. We walk towards her apartment, another Soviet-looking block surrounded on one side by a gravel pit and on the other by acres of dark grassland cut with gullies and erosion.

This is an extremely multicultural suburb, with many Latin Americans, Portuguese, Africans and *gitanos* among the Spanish. The *gitanos* around here are fine, Teresa tells me, even if many make their living "off the books" stealing and selling cars and dabbling in the drug trade.

"Many of the *gitanos* have religion and they have morals, it is fine. It's the *Kinkis* you have to worry about," she says. *Kinkis* (or *Quinquis* as it is spelled correctly) are a group of "houseless" semi-nomadic people, distinct from the Roma, who are marginalized and heavily involved in the illegal trades in the city. They are identified as mixed race *gitanos* and *gallegos* (Spanish). Teresa says they don't respect the people like those in Villaverde who might also live on the fringes.

We keep walking. It is quiet. Despite our location it is peaceful and Teresa and Isabel's presence is reassuring. Teresa lives in one of the older *torres*. The blocks either side of her building are dark, vacant expanses. The road is dirt and there are half-dressed people standing around a fire, which burns inside a 44-gallon drum; it has been repurposed as a community barbecue. Dogs stalk in packs in the shadows and the wind blows wrappers into the long grass. The upbeat rhythm and accordion riffs of Latino *cumbia* music plays from a car stereo somewhere, and the scene in front of us is only threatening when it is not understood. Teresa smiles and greets her neighbours; she asks the old lady on the corner in a wheelchair how her latest doctor's appointment went, she guides us past the crowds outside the apartment who all notice the *guiri* (Madrid slang for a blonde foreigner) arrive. We take the lift up to her small first-floor apartment; the locals call this place los *pisos*—which means "the floors" in English.

Inside we sit in the small lounge room; it is decorated with paintings of Dutch fields and Austrian lakes, images of places that Teresa has torn out of magazines and painted to brighten up the apartment she shares with her adult son. Pablo is into Tae Kwon Do and colouring *mandalas* (ritual Indian symbols) and he loves Real Madrid. He is in his mid-twenties and he has Down's Syndrome. His father left the family shortly after they found out that Pablo had a disability, baulking at the responsibility he faced. They don't receive much help and while theirs seems to be a happy life, it is a poor one. We eat slivers of white sheep's cheese and drink beer in the still room. It is noisy outside and from the window we see people wandering into the dark field next to the apartment.

"Pablo's friend was shot in the *campo*," Teresa says, as she watches me. I don't ask what happened to him. I notice a saying on one of the *mandalas* Pablo has brought to show us: "Que vivas todo el tiempo que quieras. Que quieras todo el tiempo que vivas." I'm sure it's from a commercial or slogan, though there is a sense of the city in the words: "May you live all the time you want. May you want all the time you live."

It is time to leave Teresa and Pablo in Villaverde. Isabel walks with me as I find a bus stop to head back towards the city. Wordsworth wrote of his own nightwalking in the late eighteenth century:

... the lonely roads
Were schools to me in which I daily read
With most delight the passions of mankind...

The quiet streets of Villaverde do something similar to me. This is a chance to see another side of the city, one far away from the regular view taken by outsiders. Madrid is not all Ritzy bling and royal stories. There is much more to this place at night than the histories of the city's rich and powerful. It is also home to very different people—those who live and struggle on the edges of Madrid.

Nightlife is often promoted as an intrinsic part of Madrid. Indeed, *Lonely Planet* Madrid author Anthony Ham writes that if you "Step out into the night-time streets of many Madrid neighbourhoods ... you'll find yourself swept along on a tide of people, accompanied by a happy crowd intent on dancing until dawn." This doesn't describe anywhere I've seen so far. Perhaps, I think, this is the over-enthusiasm of a guidebook writer with pages to fill, though there must be something to the truism of Madrid's nights being "the stuff of legend". Just as there is more to the city than its tourist clichés of Real Madrid and bullfighting, there must be something worth discovering with this exuberant crowd of *Lonely Planet*-inspiring *Madrileños* who are dancing until the sun comes up as well.

2am: Nightlife

Men feare death as children feare to goe in the dark.
Sir Francis Bacon, *Essayes, Civill and Morall*, 1625

"I used to be a go-go dancer," Leo Callorda tells me as he stands at the door of his nightclub in the suburbs of Madrid. He has worked in and around nightclubs as a stripper for 27 years and only recently has he decided to put his clothes back on. He is clean-shaven and fit-looking and I imagine he could step back into his old profession without a problem tomorrow if the call came.

"I'm forty-five now though, so I thought it was about time I gave it up," he says with a tinge of sadness. "My daughter kept getting asked what her daddy did for work, and I couldn't put her through having to tell her class that I was a stripper anymore," he continues as he mimes a strip, running his hands downs his sides and pouting his lips, "especially when everyone else's fathers were teachers or police officers."

We chat at the door of Leo's club, Single Love, as a stream of women in their forties get free entry down to the dark bar below us camouflaged with velvet curtains. The women are here to "restart their lives," I'm informed by the Bulgarian doorman beside Leo.

"I always loved dancing," Leo tells me as he checks ID and looks for the glassy eyes of troublemakers.

"I started dancing when I was four. By the time I was eighteen I was dancing and stripping in nightclubs to make money, and because I loved it," he says while he sips an espresso to fortify himself for the long night ahead.

Julio Iglesias plays on the speakers while drunken *divorciadas* play football in an inflatable field outside the club, hoping to stumble, quite literally, into an eligible bachelor. I see the slightly bored look in Leo's eyes; he may be a more respectable night-worker now, but he still pines for something more.

I want to experience the nightlife of Madrid in a conventional sense—to see whether the "the stuff of legend" claim is all hot air or not. Leo takes me down into his club, where the single men and women mingle in curtained off areas, sipping champagne on cushioned sun beds. There is a strange hunger in the eyes of the people, and they're clearly not here to chat with friends and dance in order to shed the stress of the week; the thick-set men gulp their gin and tonics quickly to create momentary armour; the women draped across the dark sofas tilt their heads downwards from their positions, hoping to catch the men's gaze as they walk past. Single Love is full of hunters and not enough prey. This isn't the place for me (I am neither single nor looking for the sort of love this place offers). Leo seems to want away from this place too, though he is stuck between being a respectable father and a man of the night, so he understands when I leave.

I arrive in Matadero Madrid, the city's former livestock market and abattoir, now illuminated by red lights and a lively arts and performance precinct. A friend of a friend meets me at the corner of the bridge over the Manzanares. Francisco Martínez, or Paco as his friends know him, is a local actor and director. He lived almost entirely at night here during his younger years, until his now three-year-old daughter came along and his compass changed direction. Once upon a time he would be at a club, a new bar opening, a concert or social gathering every night of the week until the last of the darkness was squeezed out by the new day.

Paco's brother is Fele Martínez, one of Spain's most famous actors, who is also one of Pedro Almodóvar's main performers; Fele has starred in films such as *Thesis*, *Bad Education* and *Open Your Eyes* with Penelope Cruz and this connection has opened many night-time doors for Paco.

He has brought his friends Miguel and Ramona along to re-live the sort of nights they used to have regularly before kids and jobs got in the way. We begin our Spanish crawl in the working-class suburb of Usera, a tightly packed mix of apartments, flat cement-floored *plazas* and family-run businesses with faded signs. Paco is excited; he loves the idea that I'm writing about his city and he regularly interrupts our conversation with the phrase "Ben, apunta" ("Ben, write this down") so he can direct the flow of our walk and the stories I capture. As with many people I meet during the night, the group I am with now seem excited that they have an excuse to revisit the hours of their youth, when things were edgier and unpredictable. It feels like the beginning of a new story for them too, one which they haven't been able to write for a while and that they'll be able to feed off for the weeks to come when they're back inside their other lives and living during the day again.

Paco leads us into a corner bar with big windows for a *caña*. This is a traditional Madrid bar and it doesn't look unlike a typical American diner, minus the kitsch, with vinyl booths and a u-shaped bar with swivel stools. The owner, Oscar, is the father of former Atlético Madrid footballer, Juanjo (Juan José Enríquez Gómez), who died recently. Oscar is 98 years old and he sits staring out of the window and folded into the corner booth with a small glass of vermouth. Another elderly gentleman sits at the bar with his "date" for the evening, a twenty-something with bright red hair and a glittering bra popping out of her top. He strokes her arm as he watches the television and she smiles distractedly while texting someone she'd rather be with. The sounds of poker machines and football fill the atmosphere. The air is thick with cigarette smoke, even though it is illegal to smoke inside bars, the suburbs work to a different rhythm. Sonia, who is behind the bar, slides an ashtray along the counter to Paco and he lights up his own cigarette. Sonia's husband is a bullfighter, though it's not as lucrative as it once was, she tells me, so she picks up shifts at the corner bar to make ends meet.

"I come in here nearly every day," Paco tells me as we sip our beers. "Oscar greets me every time as if I am a new customer. He's been doing the same for years," he says, a symptom of the owner's Alzheimer's disease.

As with the earlier *tapas* experience, we don't linger in any one place; nights out in Madrid are about maintaining momentum and energy rather than sinking into the booths of one place for the duration, as is often the Anglo custom. We must maintain the *movida* so we exit and keep moving on our unwritten itinerary.

Paco takes a phone call as we walk to the river. The water is like black glass, bubbling and slipping below us under the bridge. Paco looks at me as he chats on the phone, "Remember *golazo*, it's our password for later," he whispers cryptically.

We pass an abandoned warehouse on our right; it is where many of the heroin addicts in the city now squat. "Samur hands out methadone here," says Paco, referring to Madrid's health care service. He kicks an empty packet of the drug, which is discarded in the gutter. The Metro is finished for the night and there are no taxis so we decide to ride into the centre. One of Madrid's wonderful features is the electric bike network throughout the city. It costs fifty cents for half an hour and these white bikes can zoom through the traffic faster than most forms of public transport. There are 1,560 public electric bikes in Madrid, and from what I see as we pedal with the traffic in the dark, they are mostly well respected by the city's motorists as well. The electric kick makes riding easy and we zip around the outside of the big, sweeping roundabouts and across multilane roads that flash with the red and yellow lights of the traffic towards the looming and low-lit gates of Plaza de Cibeles in the city centre.

We dock the bikes downtown and walk the narrow lanes to Gran Vía, the most beautiful street in central Madrid. It offers the archetypal image outsiders have of the city and is the place that features on most of its brochures and postcards. It is wide and lined with a blend of majestic buildings of other eras: art-deco, Mudéjar, Vienna Secession. Elizabeth Nash captured the feeling of this wide, opulent avenue when she wrote, "Gran Vía is the pulsing aorta of Madrid, a swaggering art-deco, jazz-age boulevard lined with some of Europe's finest follies, earliest skyscrapers and glitziest movie palaces."

In 1910, fourteen surrounding streets were flattened to make way for the boulevard that would let cars drive from Cibeles to the highways that shoot off from Calle de la Princesa and in order to create a shopping thoroughfare so that Madrid could rival the cosmopolitan centres of Paris and London. Even in the early hours it is still a place full of people rolling out of theatres, bars and restaurants; I understand Nash's reference to the "pulsing aorta" as the flow of people pumps up and down the streets in an unabated stream.

Gran Vía was also a central location during the civil war, where the leftist volunteers marched along the wide bitumen in 1936 chanting "No pasarán! No pasarán!" ("They shall not pass!") in defiance of Franco's approaching forces. Later, it was where Franco concentrated his shelling to demoralize the *Madrileños* into submission. For a time during the civil war the citizens jokingly re-named Gran Vía "fifteen and a half avenue" in reference to the calibre of shells the nationalists would fire onto the boulevard at regular intervals. When Franco finally seized power in the city in 1939 he changed the famous thoroughfare's name to Avenida de José Antonio, after the executed fascist politician. After Franco's death it was restored to Gran Vía once again, while many other streets and *plazas* were likewise returned to their original names.

Gran Vía, the aorta of Madrid (Tomás Fano/Wikimedia Commons)

Paco instructs us that our first stop on the boulevard will be at Museo Chicote, which we know from the Ritz once had the longest cocktail menu in the world and a collection of 25,000 bottles in the cellar; according to Elizabeth Nash, it had everything from bottles which contained "eight drops of peppermint, to one that held 82 litres". This was the bar started by Perico Chicote, of the Ritz fame, in 1931. It was also known for its trade in black market goods—from cars and coats to medicine and apartments—and later for the *señoritas putas de derecha*, or "right-wing sluts", who would sit on the leather stools hopefully looking for company until closing time. Until recently it was also a renowned pickup joint for less salubrious types of all political persuasions.

Paco knows the current owner, a skinny hipster with black-rimmed glasses, who greets us with kisses and the admission that he's "already a little drunk". Nowadays the bar is a much more mainstream, if still exclusive, place in the inner city.

A disco ball spins from the ceiling as groups hang out in the corners and on the lounges, drinking and talking and trying to appear natural in this most unnatural setting. The wall behind the bar is full of Russian vodkas, honey-coloured whiskies from Japan, red, green and blue liqueurs and anything else a drinker could dream up. Paco orders us highball "Fernandos"—Fernet Branca and cola mixes made popular by the Argentinian expats in Madrid. The atmosphere is subdued, even awkward, until a tall, Botox-enhanced woman in her fifties with long brown hair and a flowing kaftan arrives with her entourage. Immediately she starts dancing in the centre of the room to John Paul Young's *Love is in the Air* and her group joins her without missing a beat. Paco goes up and greets the woman as she throws her hair and her hands around the room to the melody. Paco is met with an enormous hug and kisses from the pouting troupe when they recognize him in the darkness. The dancer is one of Spain's most famous flamenco singers and the man on her arm is one of the richest club owners in the city. Paco seems to be well connected.

At the end of the song Paco heads outside for a cigarette, leaving us to the bar that has been frequented by everyone from Frank Sinatra to Orson Welles. Hemingway was also a regular visitor here and he would often be found behind the bar mixing his own drinks, or, on occasion, inebriated on the floor.

Without warning there is shouting and a commotion outside. All I can see from inside the bar is a man with a white ponytail at the centre of the action; his head snaps back as a younger man punches him square in the face. The older man's nose explodes in a rainbow of snot and blood across the pavement. The red and blue flashes of a police car blend into the spinning lights of the disco ball above the bar. The car comes to a stop up on the gutter and moments later I see Paco talking to the officers while waving his hands and puffing on the last of his cigarette. The older man has his head in his hands, dripping crimson onto the cement. Behind him two women are arguing and screeching at each other, and further back I see a stocky, pensive young man leaning against the rail blowing cigarette smoke into the vacant air above his head; he is the attacker.

Through the tangle of squawked Spanish I make out that the younger woman made a comment to the older woman along the lines of "puta vieja" ("old whore") as they passed on the street; the old ponytailed man took offence and replied "vete a la mierda" ("fuck off"), to which the younger man was obliged, reluctantly, to defend his date's honour—hence the red cement outside the bar, on the aorta of Madrid. Luckily, Paco saw the whole thing; he struts between the police and the people like a lawyer on the stand.

He now has a metallic pointer with an extended index finger on the end in his hand; I have no idea where it came from, though I imagine it is one of the many props he never leaves home without. He finishes his address to the now growing crowd with an accusatory jab of the metallic hand towards the young woman. He retracts the pointer, as you would a baton or a car aerial, as if to say, "I rest my case!" The police question the younger man as they write him up a summons and an ambulance arrives to patch up the smashed nose on the pavement. Paco nods his head and leaves the bemused party outside, returning to the bar to drain the last of his drink.

The owner of Museo Chicote, now even drunker, and nearing Hemingway's favoured position on the bar's floor, thanks us all for visiting, and for containing the drama outside. He hugs and kisses us again and orders tequila shots all-round as a parting gift.

We stride up the street, *la marcha* continuing; our exploration has been energized by the action in Chicote. Next to the commotion is the quiet gentlemen's' club La Real Gran Peña, for retired military men and their associates. It contained a statue of Franco inside until 1999 and is said, ironically, to stand on the most revolutionary street corner in the city—which we have just been able to appreciate at first hand.

We walk through to the area called Malasaña. Now it is a retro and bohemian district connecting the affluence on Gran Vía to the "straight friendly" and predominantly gay *barrio* of Chueca. It was once the seediest inner suburb in the city in the 1970s and prostitution is still evident on many side streets and in darkened doorways. Eastern European and African women in high boots and little more than underwear pout at the men walking past with wandering eyes. Plaza Dos de Mayo is the centre of the *barrio* and Malasaña was also the centre of the so-called *movida madrileña* in the 1980s when the young people of the city began protesting against the Francoist legacy and its repression of everything from drugs to sex and rock and roll. This movement began with the election as mayor of the "Old Professor", as he was known, in 1979. Enrique Tierno Galván was a former professor of Marxist philosophy (expelled from the university during the Franco era), and during his seven years in office he gave Madrid permission to breathe once again. It was a place of fun and experimentation and the city began to make up for time lost during the Franco repression; Galván reinstated carnival celebrations and the city's first "festival erótico" was endorsed.

The Old Professor also created affordable housing for people in Orcasitas, Villaverde and Vallecas to alleviate the pressure on those living in slums on the edges of the city. Until his death in 1986, Galván made Madrid a place of hope and optimism for the first time in generations. It is as a result of the *movida* that Paco, Ramona, Miguel and I can enjoy the excess of nights like this.

On our march through the suburb we stop in the *plaza* for a moment. It is a strange mix of young and old; a brick archway divides the outdoor settings of the bars, and play areas are lined with a rainbow of coloured fence pickets. In the centre of the square is the statue that commemorates the only uprising by the *Madrileños* against a foreign power in their history.

After Napoleon Bonaparte staged a *coup d'état* in 1799 in France to take power, Spain's Bourbon rulers aligned themselves with the French with designs on broadening their European reach. Initially they defeated Portugal together and then declared war on their previous ally England. This led to the Battle of Trafalgar in 1805 off the southern coast of Spain where the French Navy was defeated along with Spain's hopes of ever being a world power again.

During this period a nobleman, Manuel de Godoy, had schemed his way to the top in Madrid. He was not only having an affair with the queen, but he also negotiated a treaty in secret with Napoleon for the annexing of Portugal (which was still an ally of England) whereby Godoy himself would rule one-third of the country as the "Prince of the Algarves". The treaty gave French troops safe passage through Spain on the way to Portugal, where they swiftly took Lisbon. Napoleon used this treaty to his advantage in the wake of invading Portugal. He duly revealed his grand plan, which was to remove the Bourbons and take Spain for himself. A crisis of leadership in Madrid at the time also helped Napoleon's plans.

In the face of rioting, Carlos IV abdicated from the throne in 1808 and fled straight into the waiting arms of Napoleon, who declared the Bourbon dynasty deposed and imprisoned the ex-king. Carlos' son Ferdinand VII became king briefly until the throne eventually passed to Napoleon's brother Joseph. Napoleon descended on the Spanish capital intent on removing the incumbent rulers and seizing Madrid so he could further his conquests on the Iberian Peninsula. Officially, the French were still allies of Madrid, and its citizens were told to accept the soldiers as friends and even house guests if asked, though as 10,000

French troops set up in Buen Retiro park and stabled their horses where the Plaza de Cibeles now sits, the city was on high alert. While the French showed their friendship with Madrid through rape and looting, tensions gathered.

On 2 May 1808, the last Spanish royal, the fourteen-year-old Infante Don Francisco de Paula, clattered out of the palace gates in his carriage towards exile in France. The city was abandoned by the Bourbons and the *Madrileños* revolted. General Murat, Napoleon's brother-in-law, who was charged with the offensive on the city, ordered cannons and muskets to be fired at the angry crowd while the citizens charged at the French with daggers and swords to defend their city. Rain fell as the battle began. This one-day uprising was said to be the start of the forging of modern Madrid's identity. Cannons blasted the Puerta de Alcalá, where the scars of battle can still be seen to this day, and Murat occupied the Puerta del Sol and Plaza Mayor in the hope of discouraging further rebellion. The *Madrileños* charged the invaders with sticks, antique pistols and kitchen knives; women stood on balconies and tipped pots of boiling water and rocks onto the French below who numbered between 25,000 and 35,000 in and around the city.

The Spanish troops in the capital stood by impassively, as their previous orders were to not interfere, even while the regular people defended their city. The people's ownership of their city and their role in its salvation were even demonstrated by 56 prisoners from the court prison. After pleading with their jailers they were released in order to join the battle for their city. The prisoners seized three cannons for the cause, four were killed in the fighting and, remarkably, 51 returned to their cells after the fighting: only one man absconded in the chaos in the hope of freedom after the battle. As afternoon came, the desperate people approached the artillery park (now the site of Plaza Dos de Mayo) and pleaded with the soldiers to at least open the arsenal to the people to give them a chance. Captain Luis Daoíz y Torres relented and handed out muskets, bayonets, swords and sabres to the 300 people waiting. They then set themselves up behind crude barricades with one cannon for their defence. The *Madrileños* were severely outnumbered and Murat poured thousands of soldiers at the rebels. Daoíz, another officer Pedro Velarde and their counterparts joined the people and died defending the city with them, along with 409 other locals.

Joaquin Sorolla's 1884 depiction of Pedro Velarde's death (Biblioteca Museu Víctor Balaguer/ Wikimedia Commons)

The most symbolic of these deaths was that of Manuela Malasaña, a fifteen-year-old seamstress. She volunteered to help the fighters, bandaging up men with torn bed sheets during the worst of the fighting. When Murat crushed the rebellion, an order was given to shoot any *Madrileño* carrying a weapon. As Manuela ran from the square, French soldiers, who were intent on raping her, cornered her. She lashed out with her seamstress' scissors to prevent the attack, though this was her final act, as the discovery of a weapon meant that the French had justification to execute her on the spot. Her legacy as a symbol of Madrid's spirit remains, and the *barrio* of Malasaña is named in her honour. Many of the rebels were rounded up and executed the next day by Murat's soldiers; this event is immortalized in Goya's painting *El 3 de mayo de 1808 en Madrid*. It can now be seen hanging on the walls of the Prado Museum. After the rebellion was quashed an uncomfortable truce settled on the city.

Murat left many of the dead on the streets to bloat and rot as a warning. This did not have the desired effect. Intent on seizing back their capital, the *guerrilla* fighters of the city, along with soldiers from the north and British troops under the command of the Duke of Wellesley, who did not want the French to control the peninsula, would eventually expel the French with massive casualties. This was the first battle of the Peninsular War, and it would be the offensive that would stretch the French forces and provoke the Spanish and British into fighting against a common enemy. This led to the eventual downfall of Napoleon, as he once remarked from his exile in St Helena after his defeat. In 1812 the first Spanish constitution was created and Ferdinand VII returned to Madrid in 1814 as the restored king.

Now in modern Malasaña, we continue down the cobbled lane of Calle del Barco; it is populated by drunken tourists and people lining up to enter the clubs along the street. The sex shops with dildo-clutching mannequins and BDSM chains are closed, though the man selling hot dogs next door is still open late into the night. Paco has a connection at Barco, a nautical-themed nightclub. We skip the long queue and we're admitted straight inside.

Any thoughts of sleep and tiredness are banished once we enter. Barco is pumping with dance music and the chatter of what seems like a hundred people pressed in and around the bar. Another beer is drained and while I can't hear any of the conversations around me, I can see the smiles of the sweaty, slightly inebriated people everywhere. Tomorrow, the daylight and the world outside this tiny space, doesn't exist. Maybe this is the "nightlife" that *Lonely Planet* promotes to its readers.

We occupy a narrow space in between the bar and the corridor leading to the toilets as we drink and dance. If Paco was the lawyer in the previous scenes of our night out, he is now the clown. He extends his metallic hand and blocks the doorway as a bearded man with a coiffed hairdo tries to pass. There is a moment of tension and I can see the man doesn't know what to do. Paco waits until the tension is at its peak before he moves his hips and then his head and he starts to dance to the Cyndi Lauper re-mix while still holding the hand in place. The bearded man waits a moment, the ice is broken, and he then starts dancing too. He *la bambas* his way under the hand and to the toilet, high-fiving Paco, who until a minute ago was a total stranger, on his way out.

Paco is an actor and a performer and he wears this identity with pride on our excursion. He comes from a family of actors and he punctuates our bar hopping with stories of film sets, Nicole Kidman and Almodóvar to highlight his success in more conventional realms.

From Barco we head out onto the streets again. Paco yells, "cerveza!" theatrically and within twenty seconds there is a man with a cooler on wheels selling us cold beer. This, it seems, is how the night works for the locals as they lubricate their movement from one location to the next. There are scores of Bangladeshi men walking through the busy areas during the night selling cold beers to drinkers for €1 as they move from one place to the next.

The next place on our list is Rick's on Calle del Clavel in Chueca. I've been to gay bars in plenty of cities around the world as a straight man, though there is something strange about this one. Men of all shapes and sizes lean on the bar, on the side tables, on the walls, all leering. It is that same sort of feeling I got with Single Love earlier. They're not looking at me in particular, they're looking at everyone: sizing up, checking out and mentally undressing. I suppose this is the objective of many people when they go out to bars, to find someone to "spend the night with", "sleep with" or "go home with", all nocturnal synonyms or euphemisms for the same thing. It just seems more open and apparent here. It's a crude analogy, but in this golden-lit bar with a hirsute DJ playing techno for the crowd it feels like a zoo at feeding time. Paco now plays the role of escape artist and he disentangles us from the clutches of the bar's clientele as quickly as he can. We leave to the animal looks of the men and roll back out onto the street.

Outside, people sit on benches talking, others on the edge of the gutters draining cans of Mahou beer before tossing them along the cobble stones for the cleaners. We stride up and over a pedestrian bridge past hippies smoking a *porro*—a joint. Ramona stops to chat to a girl with bare feet and she is given a joint—just as you would be given a light or directions during the day—to smoke along the road to our last stop.

Paco walks down Calle del Doctor Cortezo just outside the Tirso de Molina Metro stop. It is an unremarkable street and there is certainly no bar in sight. Paco loves the suspense as I ask what we're doing. "We'll see," he says as he approaches a peeling green door and rings the buzzer.

"What was that password again?" he asks me.

"Ah, *golazo*?" I reply, uncertain after everything that has passed since he told me.

"*Golazo…*" he croaks into the intercom. After a few minutes a man with a ponytail wearing sandals opens the door. They hug and chat, they're old friends. Miguel is his name and this is his place.

"Come upstairs," he says and we follow him up to another unremarkable door. We buzz and after a minute another man admits us inside.

It is like something from *Eyes Wide Shut*. The space is dimly lit; the walls are burgundy and hung with artwork. Curtains divide the rooms and a DJ plays chilled music from a corner of what I suppose was once the lounge room. This is an off the grid bar; it has no licence, no name and it doesn't exist except for those who know Miguel.

"Almodóvar comes here," Paco tells me as he greets famous Spanish actresses and singers. Men and women close the curtains as I walk past. I see them snort cocaine and then get up and dance in the hot, smoke-filled room, which is now packed.

Maybe Anthony Ham was right. Here there is something peculiar and intoxicating about the nightlife in its conventional sense. Unlike many other cities I've visited, the nightlife isn't about sinking as much alcohol as possible and swirling through the night in an uncoordinated fog but rather about socializing and connecting with people. Yes, drinking is part of it, though it's not at the centre of things. Pedro Almodóvar, Spain's most famous director, the son of a service station attendant from La Mancha who moved to Madrid in 1969 to start making underground movies and to challenge the monotone cultural representation of the post-Franco country, once said that "Madrid is the centre of the universe and everybody comes here to have fun."

Paco, Ramona and Miguel press into the middle of the dance floor, under the solitary air conditioner. They're smiling and I lose them in the crowd. I see the metallic pointer bobbing up and down between two women, so I know Paco is in there, somewhere. The smoke is choking me so I head down the dark corridor, past the couples making out and back down onto the street, where I'm meeting someone downstairs to walk the mazes of the city from a different perspective.

3am: Inner city walking

The day has eyes, the night has ears.
Scottish proverb

Gori Fiorentino waves his hands in the air to illustrate his story as we walk and talk along the cobbled lanes of Lavapiés. We navigate our way through the crowds of dreadlocked Rastas, Muslim men in flowing white robes and drunken revellers swaying on the footpaths. This is not normally such a busy time, though we're also here on the opening night of the Orgullo Gay festival, Madrid's Gay Pride celebration, and scores of men in singlets and neat beards are making their way through the *barrio* towards Chueca, where an impromptu party has started on the eve of the parade. We walk under lamplights and up towards the rows of cafés and bars in the centre of the *barrio*, past murals splashed on the walls: of a clown king with a lopsided crown, an enormous magnifying glass and a family, without heads, posing as if for a family portrait on the bricks of the wall. Gori begins telling me his own story and how he became a *Madrileño* as we walk through one of the most multicultural parts of the city.

"I had a friend who was a priest in Buenos Aires," he tells me as we pass bars called Lebanesa, Beirut and Hercules with customers outside smoking shishas and puffing the apple-scented smoke above their heads and into the air as the bars near closing time.

"I needed to leave Argentina and I knew people in Madrid," Gori says, after a family tragedy and the financial meltdown prompted him to look for a new life. "Because of the crisis it was very difficult for Argentinians to get accepted into Spain then."

"I'm not religious at all, though the priest could see I needed a chance to do something with my life. He knew I needed something to give me hope."

On the edge of the square, we see a group of crumpled men in dirty clothes wearing woolen hats despite the heat; they're junkies and they've just scored. Gori continues talking: "The priest lent me a set of his clothes, a bible and a white collar. I booked the cheapest flight to Madrid I could find and I had €70 left in my pocket to survive."

Echoing his story, we see the looming profile of the Iglesia San Lorenzo's peach-coloured tower illuminated by the moon, and Gori laughs: "I shaved and combed my hair to the side. I put on a pair of thick-rimmed glasses and I wore the priest's clothes to the airport." Gori now has the bronzed skin of a lifeguard and a greying summer beard.

"My mother was saying, 'Noooo, Gori, please, don't do it!'" She was worried about what the Lord might have in store for him if he went through with it.

"But I had to go," he says with finality. "I sat there, for the whole flight as a priest, talking to people and playing the role of the *padre*. The plane stopped off in Sao Paulo on the way and I remember having a beer with a few Argentinian hippies who were hoping to try their luck in Madrid the same as me. When we arrived at customs in Madrid they were the first taken out of the line and refused entry because of the way they looked. This was my only chance. I had nothing to return to. I walked toward the customs desk and put the bible down on the counter. I pulled my ticket and passport out from the pages as the officer was watching. Lucky I had thought to keep them in there."

"The officer looked me up and down and studied my passport. It was new. I didn't even have one stamp."

After an excruciating few moments, the officer nodded and stamped the first page of his passport. "He said, 'Welcome to Madrid, *padre*. Enjoy your stay.'"

Gori laughs as we pause in the centre of the *barrio*. "That was ten years ago. I've been here ever since."

We walk past the many communal seats and tables where people sit and chat or engage in games of checkers. There are Moroccans smoking cigarettes together in tight circles, darker Africans from Senegal and Nigeria adjusting their skull caps as they talk with their knees touching on the benches, there are lottery ticket sellers from Ecuador and the Dominican Republic pacing the square and Spanish grandparents from the Franco era sitting in folding chairs at the edges watching it all go by. This is the most diverse part of the city, a racial goulash all in one pot converging in the square towards which the streets named Fe (Faith), Jesús y Maria, Ave Maria and Calvario (Calvary) all converge.

This place feels as if it should have a more prominent history in the context of the city and its beginnings, and possibly a more respectable one considering the religiosity of the streets leading to its centre. Lavapiés is one of the first hubs from where new arrivals begin their transition into the city and the rest of Spain; diversity has been a part of the streets here for hundreds of years. The name Lavapiés suggests that it should have something to do with the washing of feet, though the origins of the district go back to its time as a Jewish ghetto. This ended when the 200,000 strong Jewish community in Spain, including the citizens of Lavapiés, was expelled by the *Reyes Católicos* in 1492. There was once a synagogue in the south-east corner of the square (now the site of San Lorenzo), and despite the Treaty of Granada guaranteeing religious freedom for the Jewish and Muslim populations after the *Reconquista* wars, they were banished in the name of Christian superiority all the same. Those Jews who stayed (and converted to Catholicism to survive) occupied this ramshackle suburb of twisting streets, smooth stones and *corralas* where the neighbourhood alleys open out into communal courtyards for water gathering from fountains. The Jewish people who stayed weren't prisoners, but weren't allowed to leave the boundary walls of their *barrio* either, and only four traders were permitted outside Lavapiés during the day to sell cloth and spices to the people. The night played a part here as well, as a curfew was placed on the Jewish people of Lavapiés; they were all instructed to return to their homes once it was dark, "in the same manner as the Moors" in order to maintain the "Christian harmony" of new Spain.

There was one Jew who was permitted to live outside the ghetto walls after the decree, Rabbi Jaco, who was also one of the most respected doctors in Madrid. The memory of the floods of 1434, when after seventy consecutive days of rain, drowned animals, rotting bodies and disease floated through the city streets, as well as of the great plague of 1438, was still relatively fresh, so an exception was made for the rabbi and his skills.

Lavapiés has long been a *barrio* for the underclasses and Gori tells me that in his era, when he was one of the new arrivals looking for a means to survive, it used to be a place of "rock and roll", where drug deals and dealers were common on every corner. It is now much more gentrified, though there are still rows of squatters and *piratas* as Gori calls them in vacant apartments, while flags with the white "Solidaridad" slogan printed on black material flap from balconies as Bob Marley's voice and plumes of thick smoke waft from the open windows.

As we huff up the incline Gori tells me the story of the bicycle he would ride here in the early days to help him get up the steep streets quickly as he travelled through the city between odd jobs. On one particular night he locked up his bike near the plaza: "I slotted the chain through the front wheel and around a metal bin," he says. Even that wasn't enough to stop a would-be thief. Gori returned from work to find that someone had stolen his bike and had left the wheel still chained to the bin. "It's full of *chulos* here," he says, using the Spanish term for the streetwise folk who live in Lavapiés and sell "found" goods at El Rastro market. The term is more derogatory when spoken by an Argentinian, though Gori also admits that he's been known as something of a *chulo* himself over the years.

These are the *vísceras urbanas*—the urban guts of the city, as Juan Antonio Cabezas describes them, loose and on display for all who pass through at any hour. Gori is one among many here in the *barrio bajo*—the low suburbs—both geographically and economically, for Lavapiés' sloping streets stretch down towards the river. One business which is thriving, and more common here than anywhere else I have noticed in the city, is the *locutorio*, the long distance phone exchange for people to call home. These are traditionally run by the Latin American community and are a further sign of the multicultural nature of the place.

One of the biggest draws to this area during the day is El Rastro market. This Sunday flea market is full of second-hand goods, art, old clothes, stolen items and tourist kitsch. In the eighteenth century the market was a well-established second-hand goods exchange, though as far back as the 1650s *Madrileños* down on their luck would mingle on the edges of the stinking meat market to sell trinkets, family heirlooms or carefully disguised junk to keep afloat until the next Sunday. More recently the market was made famous on an international stage by Almodóvar, who used the bustling streets in the opening of his film *Laberinto de Pasiones* as the throbbing centre of a reawakened and sexualized Madrid.

The long sloping street, Calle de la Ribera de Curtidores, where the market began was once where the slaughtered animals were dragged down into other parts of the city for processing and sale, their carcasses leaving a bloody trail on the stones—a *rastro*—and the name remains. Gori tells me that he once bought a leather jacket at El Rastro from a *gitano*, "I got a great price!" he says. It wasn't until afterwards that he noticed that it still had blood on the sleeve. It was no doubt another of the "found" items on sale, says Gori. El Rastro is one of the few places in the city where haggling is permitted and encouraged, though this is more tradition than a means to actually find a bargain. One of Gori's friends had a corner stall here once where he would sell stolen computers, but the markets are now heavily regulated so he has to conduct business in the shadows somewhere else.

At night, with the pale streetlight glow revealing only some of the secrets of the area, the sloping lanes remind me of Naples; the high apartments above us seem to lean over into the centre of the alleys as if eavesdropping on the people walking below. Washing hangs from the wrought iron balconies, and the colourful mix of the people, their drying bras, socks and underpants on show, the flags hanging from their windows and the potted plants spilling from their open windows are a kaleidoscope of sorts, telling in some sense the stories of these people, even if it is an unintentional narrative.

From a distance, the dark apartments in Lavapiés look rather like a Halloween lantern and a strange face in the night; the block of the building in front of us is illuminated by random insomniacs with their lights on. The pattern creates two lopsided eyes high up, further down there is a rectangular nose where I can see a middle-aged man on his computer, and down low, maybe on the second floor, is the mouth—it is an entire apartment open and lit up with a party still pumping. The people lean over from the balcony like jagged teeth from the mouth, wriggling and laughing from its opening.

Gori knows this suburb well and he is very fond of it, though his entry stamp into Madrid wasn't the ticket to paradise that he had hoped for. Spain didn't roll out a welcome mat for him and he was soon skipping meals and picking up off-the-books jobs just to survive. Gori is as much strolling down his own memory lane as taking me on a walk through the inner city in the early hours. He lived and worked around the centre for many years handing out pamphlets, working in bars, as a lifeguard, and even making money as a "clapper" in the studio audiences of local TV shows to survive. When his work dried up, though, "at around this time of year," he saw an advertisement for the forthcoming Gay Pride festival and the famous running race, *La Carrera de Tacones*, for transvestites in stilettos, which would net the winner €600. This meant the difference between survival and retreat back to Argentina for Gori, so he borrowed a dress and entered the race. He was to run the *carrera* as a short, straight man against the most athletic transvestites in Spain so that he could eat and pay his rent. "I borrowed some high heels and I was in the race."

It is well after 3am, yet the place is still full of life. Three men in long, colourful robes float down the hill, a toddler pushes her pink pram past a sleeping man and the smell of marijuana sits like fog above the outdoor benches where people are drinking *cañas* of beer, even if it is after closing time.

"I'm not gay. But I had to run. I had no choice," Gori continues. "All the other competitors were admiring their dresses and gossiping. I was doing my stretches and looking at the course."

He rakes his foot against the cobbles like a bull. "I rubbed down the edges of my stilettos too so I could run properly. My future depended on it."

As if on cue we see a gaggle of impeccable transvestites with long legs and blonde hair crossing towards Chueca.

"The gun went off and I sprinted," he recalls as he props his elbows out like weapons. "It was an obstacle course and at the first station I slipped into the evening dress with a big lead. I got my wig on at the second and then I smeared on the bright red lipstick at the third," he continues, now laughing at the memory. "I was neck and neck with an English guy and then Poww! I shoved him out of the way on the home straight and I thought I was going to win the €600 prize."

"And what happened?" I ask, getting in my first words for a while.

"A *travesti* came from nowhere and won the race," he says, seeming disappointed for the first time tonight. He perks up: "But I got second place and they gave me €200. With that money I could pay my rent and I could stay in the city," he concludes as we walk towards the beginnings of this year's Gay Pride festival. "It's been ten years since I ran the *carrera* at my first festival; and I've been here ever since."

On the way to Chueca we stop at a rainbow-painted hole in the wall. Most places have city orders to close their doors at 3am, though there are still bars that persist after this. Inside the Maloka bar there is a solitary man on a stool at the back playing a ukulele and four people gyrating on the tiny dance floor. This is a Brazilian gay bar and the walls are filled with flags, black figurines dancing and Diego Rivera-esque pictures. This is one of the beautiful things about the night in Madrid; this tiny three-metre-square bar is just as interesting and important as the big nightclubs, the

Carrera de Tacones, 2015 (tedeytan/Wikimedia Commons)

tapas joints and the flamenco performances. They're open late to celebrate the gay festival and the owner passes around thimbles of *cachaça*, the sugarcane liquor of her home country.

Chueca is named after Federico Chueca, a writer of *zarzuela* (a type of musical drama typical of Madrid). He was born in the city in 1846 and, while he wasn't gay, his love of the arts has transitioned well into the modern rendering of his *barrio*. Chueca is located in the central district next to Gran Vía, with its limits drawn by the Calle del Barquillo and Calle de Fuencarral. Chueca enjoys a privileged location now, and as such it is one of the most expensive places to live in the city. Even though it is now modern and cosmopolitan, in the 1970s and 1980s before the democratic transition it was one of the most dilapidated and dangerous parts of the city; like Malasaña and Lavapiés, it was centred on drugs and prostitution in the wake of Franco's repression.

Further along the route to Chueca the streets are quiet as Gori and I walk. There are no cars on the cobbled lanes and the only person we see is an old man in his *relojería*—watchmaker's shop—still at work winding back time for customers. We continue walking and gradually we begin to hear a roar at the top of the hill. The noise and the congregations of people increase until we arrive at the *plaza* in Chueca. Once a sinister place of drugs and illicit sex, it wasn't until the *movida* of the 1980s and the adoption of the area by the gay community that the district was transformed into the colourful and most progressive part of Madrid.

We hear it before we see it. The Plaza de Chueca is full to bursting. It is the first night of the Gay Pride festival, and all the revellers have come to the *plaza* for an impromptu party. Tomorrow the floats will travel down the Paseo del Prado and there will be more than 100,000 people watching on as the biggest and brightest are on display. Tonight, there must be 10,000 men, women, transvestites and transsexuals together drinking summer red wine with large ice cubes sloshing the candy-coloured *vino* onto the pavement. Bangladeshis walk through the crowds with plastic bags selling cans of beer as people sit on strips of cardboard chatting and drinking. We walk past shops like the Viva El Musculo store selling muscle tops and short shorts and SR Leather offering all sorts of add-ons and accompaniments to the discerning shopper.

Madrid is one of the friendliest LGBT cities in the world, and Chueca is at the centre of it all. As one of the many progressions after the *movida* of the 1980s, Spain is one of the most open places in Europe: gay marriage has now been recognized for ten years, gay people are allowed to serve openly in the military, adoption is legal, and there is an estimated LGBT population in greater Madrid of 500,000. It is said that this attitude stretches back to ancient times when the Romans, who had an open attitude to sexual interaction and homosexuality, travelled to the Iberian Peninsula.

In Chueca, and all of Madrid at this time of year, the rainbow flag of the gay community is visible flapping in *plazas* and at open windows. The colours of the flag have significance as well: red means life, orange health, yellow signifies the sun, green harmony with nature, while blue represents art and violet symbolizes the spirit.

The origin of this neighbourhood in its current incarnation could begin in one of the most famous cafés in the city: the Gran Café de Gijón. The Gijón started in 1888 outside the city. It was a place where many celebrities met—literary types, artists, singers and politicians. When it moved to Paseo de Recoletos it continued to be one of the meeting points for the city's artists and writers during and after the civil war. Some of the homosexual writers and artists would also frequent nearby streets, Prim and Almirante, to meet other clandestine artists for trysts in relative safety. Gay prostitution was also centred around the café during this period, conducted in the *pensiones* and *hostales* in the area.

In Chueca's *plaza* we walk past the public toilets, ordinarily not a significant tourist stop, though these toilets were part of a social revolution; it has been said that they were the place at which many gay people met up clandestinely, especially as homosexuality was illegal during the Franco years. Because the gay community used to congregate around the *baños* some of the first gay-oriented businesses in the city opened here—and now the nightclubs B&W and Rimmel Pub have opened just across from this former hotspot in recognition of its past importance.

Chueca's identity was forged after the political oppression that led to the *movida*. The post-Franco period was a time of liberation throughout Spain, and the gay community began its struggle for respect and recognition on the streets of this formerly destitute *barrio* in Madrid.

Regardless of its reputation, homosexuals felt safe here due to its relative isolation from the more conservative and aggressive aspects of society. Gradually, as gay-friendly businesses such as the radical Berkana bookshop opened, it became a place where gays and lesbians could live and feel part of a wider society. In 1977 Chueca was widely recognized as a gay neighbourhood, transformed into a space for gay-centred leisure, though also one that was respectful of the rest of the city. This new identity also created many commercial opportunities, from bookshops and clothing stores to restaurants and saunas. The resulting relative safety led to the gay community here beginning the fight for its rights on a broader scale. It made the *barrio* famous as the centre of many important campaigns for homosexual recognition in Spain. Nearby Calle Pelayo is where the Orgullo Gay began fifteen years ago, and gay tourism has become a significant success story as one of the most engaged modern examples of gay recognition and rights in the world.

Aside from the bars, sex-shops, saunas and themed book stores one thing I notice on fliers and in shop windows is the *triángulo rosa*. The pink triangle was originally marked on gays to identify and stigmatize them during Hitler's period in power in Germany. The mark was sown onto the clothes of people suspected of being gay, in some cases along with yellow symbol denoting their Jewish identification. Around 220,000 gays and lesbians died among the six million who were exterminated by the Nazis during World War II as part of Hitler's "final solution". Since 1970 the pink triangle has become a symbol that recognizes the importance of the homosexual movement towards equality. It is also used to remember the atrocities the gay community endured during the war and to emphasize the solidarity of today's gay movement.

From Chueca we walk through the centre towards Gori's old street, Echegaray where he lived in an apartment with eight others near the Teatro Español, where he eventually met his wife. It is now full of drunken foreigners and women pushing pamphlets and vouchers into our hands for free drinks at their clubs and strip joints, which will still be open for hours to come. The Plaza de Santa Ana is quiet; the statue of Lorca is now alone for a few hours until the sun comes up. What I notice from our walk is that the centre of Madrid is quite small. Without the heat of the day and with the aid of more than a few *cañas* of beer we have navigated the early history and the modern reality of the city in a matter of hours. Even at night this place is alive. How busy it is surprises me. When I began this exploration I was expecting dark corners and dubious characters. Seeing octogenarians using the pedal machines and ten-year-olds eating ice cream while they roller blade through the streets breaks this preconception apart, though I think that this is part of getting to know a city when you're an outsider. What others have written, whether in literature or tourist guides, helps to form your image of a place, and it's not until you stray from the lines written by others that you form your own narrative of a city. I know that in the case of Gori's hometown, Buenos Aires, its image as a multicultural, troubled and magical place was created by my reading everything from Bruce Chatwin to Borges before I arrived. It wasn't until I lived there that I created an image of the city for myself. It became a place of late nights, close family and long lunches in the suburbs. This is what I hope to do tonight, to create my own image of Madrid after dark that I can capture and remember, one different from my own preconceptions, from the guidebook view and from the idiosyncratic narratives that visiting writers such as Hemingway and Gerald Brenan have created in different eras.

Gori and I continue walking beyond the party, which shows no signs of abating. All through these inner city areas at night there are African migrants selling to tourists; they stand on corners and along the edges of thoroughfares with thick, white sheets with a long rope attached to each corner called a *manta*. On the sheets they have hats, replica football shirts, sunglasses and fake handbags. The ropes, I see, are for when the police who aren't getting a kickback arrive. The men are always holding their displays by the four ropes and as soon as trouble arrives, they yank the ropes together, coiling their goods into a bundle so that they can run to the next location without getting stung with a fine.

On the streets tourists continue to tumble out of bars into the alleys, street cleaners hose the rubbish of the day off the pavements and street sellers lug their bags home until the morning's shift begins. They're all crossing the same space and showing the connection that exists here after dark.

We continue walking and it is easier to find truly dark spaces now; quiet alleys to piss in, streets with no electric light, and rows of apartments closed up and black. In this state as Gori and I walk, I begin to see things more clearly, the blobs of blackness take shape. I see the gargoyle above in a church's alcove, a bicycle hiding behind a skip bin ahead and the faint colour differences of the red brick walls of the alleys.

Night vision is like this for all humans; our eyesight improves at night as our pupils dilate, sucking every sliver of light in from the world. It is said that at night, our peripheral vision improves; we see the rustle in the bins at the end of the street, the flapping clothes on a balcony above and the man in shorts drinking tea at his window. Humans are said to have better night vision than most animals, who rely on their other, sharper senses, and, surprisingly, consuming alcohol, though not to excess, also improves night vision.

So far, this is the most electric hour of the night, as many people are in the final act of their nocturnal adventures—the climax of their story for the evening. It's hard not to be swept up in the energy of the place. Very rarely do I live through a night where I'm only in the moment and not thinking about tomorrow and putting the brakes on. Tonight is such a night, though I get the impression that it is a common thing for many people here.

We continue walking back to Plaza Mayor, where I was only hours before. I see a later sort of reality in Madrid's most famous landmark. Windows are shuttered and the slight breeze raises the day's rubbish from the gutters where homeless people sleep inside cardboard boxes pressed against the 500-year-old cobblestones. I see one apartment still lit up and open for the city to see inside; it is painted deep red inside, there is a large, black piano in one corner and a chandelier above it. People from those same windows have witnessed royal weddings, civil wars, bullfights, heretic burnings and hangings, and this is just another night where they are witness to the passing of time.

The square is quiet and haunted now. The pavements are being hosed and it is beautiful. The light glints from the water on the stones and I'm surprised how much the plaza has changed in a few hours. There are couples sleeping in the corners, a few waiters cleaning up and other nightwalkers crossing the square. This is 2016, though for a brief moment it feels like it could be any time.

Gori breaks the silence telling me how he's survived and thrived here. "I can't stop talking to people," he says. It is his way of connecting and working people out. He still struggles financially and works as a pool lifeguard, though his social networks are rich here. "It's who I am," he says.

"See that church there?" he asks me. It is the rose-coloured Iglesia Santa Cruz. "I once went in during a wedding, to talk to people when I arrived because I was lonely. I wasn't a wedding crasher, I just wanted some company."

"I used to stand next to bus drivers and chat until they put up the yellow line," he adds. Talking was his way of making sense of the city, just as walking is mine now. We continue along the steep Plaza de la Paja, a place nearly always in the shade during the day because of the buildings leaning over the rustic-feeling square. It is now empty and the shadows of the trees use the street lamps to stretch to the stones that were once part of the very first *plaza* in Madrid.

We walk towards the streets of La Latina, I've been here before, though now it's a different place. It's older, the noises and sights of technology are absent and all we see as we trace back down the Calle de Cava Baja are the big, wooden doors, the stones, the orange lanterns and the bins. It feels as if it would be just as natural to see a horse clopping past, or a resident emptying his latrine bucket onto the road as it would be to see a scooter or a drunken Irishman urinating behind a bin. We're as much taking a temporal walk in the city as a geographical one. At each hour the tone, the noise, the feel of the streets shift and change slightly.

Gori's hippy soul shows itself when we pass an overflowing dumpster. On the top of the pile he sees eight or ten shoe boxes. When he opens them and looks inside he finds loafers, some newish trainers, a pair of smart sandals and some shoes he'll give to his daughter. It's the highlight of the night for him and he's surprised that this sort of bin diving isn't more popular here, "Look at these!" he exclaims, showing me the mostly new loafers, "I'll wear these tomorrow!"

We walk past Carrera de San Jerónimo—it is all wood and stone, haunting and beautiful in the orange dark. In the alleys there is blackness, though the rest of the night in the city is pale orange from the diffused streetlights.

It is only now, as 4am approaches, that Gori reveals to me that he has to work in the morning. It is a common thing for *Madrileños* to push into the night like this and to not make a big deal of it. He had a siesta after work and he'll have another after finishing his work at the pool tomorrow. Sensing that our time together is up, Gori leaves me at Plaza de Cibeles to continue my exploration. He's going home and I'm getting on a bus.

4am: The *buho*

Every large city is a little world.
François-Victor Fournel

Expanding on the insight of the nineteenth-century observer of Parisian street life, Ted Conover writes in *Routes of Man*, his book on the impact of roads in different cities around the world, that "every road is a story" within its own microcosm. Cities are connected by their roads and sometimes consumed by them. The urban architecture of a city, which includes and accompanies roads, accounts for 50 per cent of all land in Los Angeles and 25 per cent in London, according to Iain Borden in the collection of essays *Restless Cities*. Look at the congestion on the looping motorways and winding freeways of Bangkok's constipated centre at any time of day or night, or the reliance which every vehicle, from transport lorries through to bicycle rickshaws, has on the main thoroughfare which cuts Bangladesh's capital, Dhaka, in two. Even if the slow and indirect way of the *flâneur* is a more measured means to see a city, the road is unavoidable.

In Madrid it is no different. The public transport on Madrid's roads is the blood that pulses along the city's veins, keeping it alive through the night. While the Metro here is one of the largest networks in Europe, between 2am and 6am it pauses to catch its breath. This is when the *buho*, or "owl", network of night buses which travel the city's roads after midnight continues to keep Madrid's heart beating. While experiencing the roads of our own city through the frame of a car's window might be the norm, in these early hours of the day in Madrid the road is a place for the passenger—and the commuter.

Rachel Bowlby writes in *Restless Cities* of commuters who use trains and buses to travel between home and work and to separate these two lives. They are supposed to be programmed and predictable, "unthinking in his daily A to B to A, up and down, round and round". I think this is the same lens through which the travellers at the airport viewed their surroundings, or rather saw through them as they journeyed towards their end point without ever really noticing the things around them. The commute is a mechanical process, not an imaginative one. The regular on the bus is not supposed to, "see or smell or feel the city as a source of wonder or stimulation, but only as a means to an end". So if I am an outsider, a temporary traveller on a bus in this place, I wonder what it makes me except someone who momentarily doesn't belong. "The commuter is the city's antithesis to the *flâneur*," continues Bowlby. Commuters are travellers of straight lines and known paths, the exact opposite of what I've done so far tonight.

In Madrid, the night buses all leave from the central Plaza de Cibeles. The fountain spurts up in the centre of the roundabout as cars pass under the nearby gates of the Puerta de Alcalá. There are workers heading out and coming home, party-goers sleeping it off in doorways or gearing up to begin their night before it is too late, all waiting to use Madrid's night owl service.

The opulent Cibeles square used to be the point of separation between the royal palaces and the urban sprawl. The axis was created in 1570 and in its middle is a statue of the Phrygian goddess Cybele astride a chariot being pulled by two prowling lions as if through the puddles of a storm— the water is lit at night and the spray changes from blue to pink and then yellow as I approach. This is also the symbolic centre of celebration for the fans of Real Madrid when yet another title or cup is won.

I want to experience the nightlife of the road in Madrid, but I also want to sit for a while and digest everything I've seen and done so far.

Bus drivers stand around chatting and gossiping, holding their clipboards and thermoses and waiting until their shift begins; the *kiosco* which sells newspapers and tourist maps is boarded up and the stairs of a nearby building are full of people waiting until their *buho* arrives. I smell sour alcohol and vomit, though most people look nothing other than sober and tired.

There are buses going to every corner of Madrid; I will go to a new area and I want to leave soon so I decide I'll take the next bus which opens its doors for passengers: it is the N3 which will take me to Canillas in the north-east. I pay my €1.50 fare and enter the bus with six or seven others. I take a seat, semi-concealed from the driver behind an advertising board and near the rear door as we twist out and around the roundabout and into the streets.

The bus ride is quick and bumpy; the seats are greasy. I peer out of the scratched window to get my bearings and see the Goya Metro stop, though there is nothing else I can recognize. It reminds me how valuable walking is, allowing you to go slowly and absorb a place, rather than losing it in a montage of blurred urban scenery while you think about other things. Walking at night permits you to make sense of the streets a little more, from the source of the noise at the end of the alley through to the reasons why you're out there on the pavement in the first place.

We drive past Calle de Alcalá, then Martínez de Izquierdo and up Avenida de Bruselas. They pass quickly, with only flashes of landmarks to identify where we're going. There are 27 stops on this journey and I want to sit through them all.

Soon we pass the Museo Africano Mundo Negro where visitors during the day can enter to experience the African history and culture that have been created in the city as well as the art, music and masks of sub-Saharan Africa. There is a long history of an African presence in both Madrid and Spain: from the Muslims who first arrived from North Africa in 711 through to the scores of mostly young men from Nigeria, Senegal and Mali among many other places who now stand on the corners of the most popular streets in Madrid selling imitation goods to survive. Spain's presence within Africa, a history of occupation and colonialism, mostly now echoes of the past. Yet there is still an interesting example of how Spain's legacy in Africa persists in the two "exclaves", Ceuta and Melilla, which are essentially Spanish outposts and semi-autonomous communities surrounded by Moroccan land and which fall under the same jurisdiction as those in Madrid or Valencia. Ceuta is on the northernmost tip of Morocco, facing Gibraltar across the strait of the same name and only forty kilometres or so from Algeciras in Spain. The other exclave along the Moroccan coast to the east is Melilla, with a population of 77,000 people. In recent years it has seen hordes of desperate people either trying to cross the treacherous waters from Morocco in flimsy rafts and dinghies or trying to scale the six-metre high fences that ring Melilla to find asylum and sanctuary in Spanish territory. I am sure that many of the young men I have seen tonight with their *mantas* of football shirts and sunglasses have arrived in Madrid via this route. I doubt whether many of these stories are told in the museum, though they are worth considering nonetheless.

Along the wide road I see that there is still the odd tourist riding an electric bike through the city streets despite the hour. A man with a vintage mullet hairstyle and a tanned young woman get on at the next stop. They wear identical blue uniforms and they look like they've just finished their shifts. This is the nightlife of the majority of people in the city, not the Museo Chicote or a Real Madrid game. It highlights an interesting aspect of being a visitor to a city. When we visit, we're often looking for the "highlights" of a place, though whose highlights are these? There is a strange sense of tourist construction to it all. In my home city, Adelaide, I know that the highlights that are thrust upon visitors are very different from the reality when you live in a place.

Despite the mundane view through the window of "real" Madrid, taking a bus into the outer suburbs in the early hours is really the only time my imagination allows me to be a little fearful. It's the first time I can decompress and think a little. I was warned of taking the wrong *buho* in the early hours; Gori told me that if I took the wrong line I'd get home wearing nothing but my underpants.

Around stop 12 or 13 of the journey two young guys get on the bus. They sit right behind me and I can smell the wine on their breaths. They laugh in that way young people do when they've got an audience; it's

A lonely bus on Madrid's ring road (Luis García/Wikimedia Commons)

more of a cackle and they lean in to see what I'm doing—this strange *guiri* with a notepad. I'm a little scared, though I think it's a combination of things: it's the first time someone has shown an uncomfortable interest in what I'm doing during the night, which is surprising, and it's also the first time my presence has stood out because I'm alone. I also realize that apart from my tiredness, the fear is probably due to the fact that I'm in a foreign place, I'm the "other" here and so the threatening potential of the unknown is amplified. If I sat on a late night bus in my own city it wouldn't even rate a mention. As we turn right through a winding suburban street of darkened houses it also makes me think of travel writing and how the position of many writers when they are "on the job" is to search for these sort of situations, where there is a flirtation with danger and the unknown in order to create more exciting anecdotes for the reader, even if truthfulness is stretched in the process. As if the two youths could decipher my scribbles, which conclude that there won't be a robbery or abduction on board tonight, they stumble off the bus at the next corner without giving me a second glance.

We continue and people gradually get off and disappear in the darkness towards home. They're all looking out of the window for the familiar signs of home—the street number on a gate, the white van in the driveway or the black painted stairs at the entrance to an apartment block. They're looking through the journey towards their destination, much like those people at the airport who weren't really there in the way that those who slept the night in the same place were. I have no stop to get off at, I don't know where I'm going, and so I just sit and wait for something to happen. And then I'm the last one on the bus. We're not in a *bajo* area, there are nice cars parked on the streets, apartments, manicured trees and clean *plazas*. I'm still waiting for the last stop and I don't know what I'll do when I arrive. Maybe I'll find a place to wait out of view until the next bus comes along, whenever that might be.

After a few minutes things start to look familiar and I wonder if it's a sleep hallucination. The Goya Metro appears again, I see the same old lady sitting under the lights of a park bench I saw forty minutes ago and the same corner piano bar with metallic chairs stacked out in front. We pass through a succession of green lights and build up speed going back the way we came. While I was preoccupied with what my next move would be and what I'd do at the end of the line, without realizing it and with the bus driver not noticing me, I've done the circuit and I'm now heading back towards the Plaza de Cibeles. The bus is busier now as we near the last stop; kids around me plan an impromptu party at someone's house, though first they decide to drink on the steps outside the "Chino" before they make their next move.

I'm starting to fade. I have powered through the night with a mix of curiosity, alcohol and adrenaline, though my head begins to fill with sand once again. It is the tiredness behind my eyes trying to seep out and lull me to sleep. It's been more than 24 hours since I've slept now and as we lurch around corners I do feel the urge to vomit. Because I'm a father of two young children, though, I'm also well trained in the technique of fighting sleep deprivation so I can swallow it back down and continue looking out of the window at the city with its curtains drawn.

The thoughts of tiredness remind me of a tragically afflicted family in Venice I had read about. I think about sleep as my eyes glaze over at the streetlights and dark avenues of Madrid. I am awake only for a night to experience a city and this is insignificant in the broader scheme of things. According to the Australian Broadcasting Corporation, parents in Australia lose up to 750 hours of sleep a year with new babies. Even still, this is nothing; imagine if you caught a prion parasite that meant that you couldn't sleep ever again, until it killed you. Fatal Familial Insomnia is a rare inherited prion disease linked to bovine spongiform encephalopathy ("mad cow disease") and Kuru. It was first noticed in the highlands of Papua New Guinea in the 1950s when scientists discovered a disease in which victims would deteriorate in middle age into a permanently sleepless state that after nine months would kill them. They later linked this condition to the rogue prions passed by the eating of dead relatives (never a good idea), though it has continued to show up, most recently in D.T Max's exploration of the disease in *The Family That Couldn't Sleep*, in which he investigates the disease within a noble Venetian family who have suffered over generations from lethal insomnia. This is still an incurable illness, and it is thought that up to 200 families around the world are awake, right now, still tormented by sleeplessness.

While my mind is wandering I don't notice the bus pull back into the Cibeles interchange. I don't want to do the loop again so I stumble out into the street again, not really sure what to do next. Despite my fears at this early/late hour in the "dead of the night", when the sky is at its blackest and the night seems vast, I also realize how safe Madrid is. I have been exposed to all sorts of uncertainties so far and nothing has happened to threaten my safety even slightly.

The drivers are still milling around outside their buses in the minutes leading up to their scheduled departures. I consider going somewhere else on the *buho*, this time maybe to the south or the east of the city where the slums are. I take a seat on the stairs for a moment to see what comes along first.

While I'm waiting, I sit with the others who are coming and going in the night: drunken party-goers, tired workers with untucked shirts and odd loners, like me, who aren't categorized quite as easily. After a while I notice the build-up of white and red taxis on the edge of the *plaza*. One driver waves at me as I stand and his movement gets my attention. He asks if I need a ride. I wait a moment to consider this proposition, and then I nod and approach the taxi.

5am: Taxi

Let there be light...
Genesis 1:3

"Are you talkin' to me?" yells Vicente through the open window of his taxi.

"Areeee youooo tawkin' to meeeee!?" he shouts, opening his lungs and echoing Travis Bickle, the infamous creation of Robert De Niro in the film *Taxi Driver*. In the process Vicente startles the patrons of one of Madrid's swankiest clubs as we drive past in the early morning dark. Bickle suffered from the same insomnia as Charles Dickens, but rather than walking he drove through the streets of his city, New York, to allow his paranoid fantasies to take shape.

I am with *Madrileño* Vicente Sanz as he takes me on a taxi tour of his city in the last hour of full darkness. He's bald, with large eyebrows and a big smile; he's a modern-day Spanish taxi driver without the Bickle issues. Every Friday and Saturday he works from midnight until 6am and he wants to give me a taste of the life of a taxi driver at night here. Vicente is only thirty years old, though he's already been behind the wheel of a taxi in Madrid for eight years. His father was a taxi driver and in his first few years he worked for him, before saving to buy his own plate and taxi licence.

"I like the tradition of the job, I like driving and I like talking to people," he says, explaining why he fell into his father's profession so easily.

I don't really have a plan of what I want to do, or where I want to go. We will take a circuitous route, letting chance and inspiration direct where we turn, as I have requested. Vicente offers to just start driving and we'll see where we end up. We drive past the viaduct—Las Vistillas—and over a bridge enclosed by a Perspex fence higher than two metres. Vicente sees me looking at this modern health and safety barrier with curiosity. "Once I was driving on the road below this and someone jumped off the bridge into the traffic. He hit a *panadero*—a bread truck—and the impact killed the driver of the truck, though the jumper survived. It was a famous suicide spot. Now they've blocked off the edges of the bridge so it's not dangerous for those below on the highway as well."

We drive through the night streets in the direction of Lavapiés and he tells me that the biggest burden of being a taxi driver is the sheer hours involved: he works fifteen hours a day during the week and then until 6am on Friday and Saturday to pay off the €173,000 fee he paid for his taxi licence.

"My parents' house cost less than my taxi licence," he tells me, though he's happy to have work, when so many don't in Madrid. He averages €200 a night in fares, which gradually chips away at his debt.

The dark streets are still populated: people sit on the stairs of a library passing a litre bottle of beer along the line as they take a swig, while men wearing basketball caps still sell hashish in the little lanes off from the main *plaza* which I walked through only hours before. While there are fewer vehicles at this time of the night, I notice that the vacant roads are an excuse for young men on motorbikes and fast cars to open the throttle through the tunnels and four lane roads in attempts to street race or impress passengers. Even so, Vicente has never had a car crash in eight years and he's only ever seen one in all that time; he's also never been robbed during his night-time drives through the city.

"Many times people have run out of the taxi and not paid, twice I got out of the taxi and chased them down the street and tackled them. They paid up after they realized I could call the police if I wanted; mostly they're just drunk and being stupid," he says, not seeming too bothered that it's something his passengers try to get away with.

During the economic crisis here he had every motivation to chase down his fares, as he used to earn about half what he does now. "And this went on for seven years," he adds, before telling me that it is starting to get better now and there is more stability in the city.

Vicente's has had all sorts of people in his taxi: prostitutes making house calls, a lady giving birth once and even a threesome of revellers who got a little too amorous in the early hours and were completely *desnudos* in the back seat of his cab before he dropped them at a hotel.

The stream of the orange, red and white city lights and the ticking of the engine lull me momentarily. We don't talk for a few minutes, and I don't ask where we're going, I just watch out of the window as we pass through the city's buildings and the ever present glow of the streetlights. At a traffic light next to a bridge I see a group of people curled together on greying mattresses and covered haphazardly with torn sleeping bags in the alcoves of the structure. This makes me wonder how they got here; my mind flicks to my children for a moment and I wonder what someone would do if all their luck came crashing down and if they had a family to worry about in Madrid. Where would they go during the night? Vicente says he'll show me later on when we drive to the extremities of the city.

Despite Madrid being a remarkably safe place so far, there are areas which I can't visit at night: because they're dangerous and I don't know where I can and can't enter safely; because I'm a foreigner and I would sometimes be a target; and also because the distances to some areas are simply too far to attempt on foot. This is where I will use the taxi to explore some of the outskirts I wouldn't otherwise be able to reach.

I ask about the red light district, the *zona roja*, and Vicente scoffs. I didn't take him for someone with a place on such moral high ground. We drive through the *plaza* in Lavapiés where people still sit on the benches in the warm early morning, mostly drunks and junkies now.

"Here is the *zona roja*. It's full of communists," he says dismissively of the square. "I'm not sure what's so interesting about *comunistas* for you anyway?" I laugh at the miscommunication: "I meant the other *zona roja*, you know *prostitutas*…", wanting to see how this aspect of life fits into Madrid, which seems to me to be as modern as any European capital, though with many of the same frayed edges and issues as developing countries in Latin America. Recent statistics have also cited Spain as having the largest number of prostitutes in Europe (upwards of 300,000), most in bordellos, and with €3.8 billion spent as recently as 2014 on prostitution, I'm sure that some people do have to operate on the edges and without the relative protection of the health monitoring that occurs in the more organized centre.

Vicente nods and programmes his GPS: "Ahh, this is no problem." We drive south along the wide and lonely main roads, out past Villaverde and the edge of the city to a place called Colonia Marconi. Behind the Metro station is a series of looping roads and roundabouts which head downhill into an industrial estate. A police car pulls out from a corner and follows us for a moment before overtaking and speeding into the night to a more pressing call. This is the first area of the more dangerous *barrios* in Madrid, Vicente says, including Orcasitas and Villaverde. We keep driving downhill past the locked gates of factories into Marconi. Among the car parks and scrub there are scores of prostitutes in the semi-darkness illuminated by the orange streetlights. They wait for the passing cars to slow down and they pout, dance or approach the open windows.

Despite the strangeness of this street, it is one of the quietest places I've been in the Madrid night so far. There are shrubs and stands of gnarled trees all around and tracks littered with rubbish leading into the complete blackness behind us. Cars are parked on the side of the road; I see a head bobbing up and down in the fogged windows of a van and a silver car with its lights off cruising the "Latina" lane. Up ahead is a woman sitting in the gutter listening to her iPod. She is completely naked apart from her stilettos and she tunes out the rest of the world and nods along to the music as if doing nothing more serious than waiting for a bus. Samur, Madrid's health service provider, does monitor the goings on here, though like many things, it is a place where a see no evil, hear no evil attitude prevails. It seems that most people are content enough to ignore the issue of prostitution when there are larger and more publicized problems such as unemployment and political corruption.

"All this is controlled by the Russian mafia," remarks Vicente. "They all used to be in the Casa de Campo (the enormous park in the west of the city) though the government 'cleaned up' the problem and they all moved here."

Further along there must be twenty women in a row: Russian, Romanian, Ghanaian and Dominican. Each street has a theme and Vicente points out their pimp, *el jefe*—a wiry man with a crewcut who is purposefully pushing a shopping cart along the streets as he checks on those who answer to him. The man twitches as he walks and hunches his shoulders, a sign of ice or cocaine in his blood, Vicente thinks. I wonder what he's doing with the trolley, though I doubt he's handing out refreshments and clean towels to his workers. I would like to talk to one of the women to hear her story, where she's from and how she got here, but as we wind the window down one blonde lady offers a variety of services ranging from €15 up to €100 to come home with us in the back of the taxi. I then see the pimp in the background and I realize it's an impossible and inappropriate place to ask such questions. We pass a collection of parked cars with foggy windows and I signal Vicente to move us along.

As we drive up and out of Colonia Marconi we talk about Uber, the new private transport option for customers that now has private cars in 250 cities around the world. After operating briefly in Madrid under the

UberPop name, whereby drivers could assume the role of a taxi with no official licence and very few background checks, it has now been outlawed by the Spanish government. Protests from the various taxi organizations in the city led to Uber being declared illegal (mostly over licensing), though Vicente is still worried about the future. He estimates that there are around 15,000 taxis in Madrid and many people would lose their jobs if Uber was legalized; it's a worry that isn't going away.

"We're very scared," he says of the new dynamic it may bring. "For all the money my licence cost, maybe I should sell it and buy a Ferrari and then drive for Uber before it's too late. I'm sure I'd get lots of work," he says as we pass the green cross of an all-night *farmacia*.

Now back in the city proper, we drive past the richest suburb of inner Madrid, Salamanca, and the temple of Real Madrid, the Santiago Bernabéu stadium. It is a wedding cake arena of concrete ribs and soaring staircases leading inside the home of Europe's most famous football team. This stadium, which can accommodate 81,044 people, was built during Franco's first era of repression in 1947. It is a powerful symbol of the "era

The Santago Bernabéu stadium (Little Savage/Wikimedia Commons)

of evasion" when people would throw themselves into supporting Real Madrid in order to suppress the misery that Franco had created beyond the pitch. It is also worth remembering that this enormous stadium was built at a time when people were starving and employment was scarce. The Santiago Bernabéu is named after the club's most famous president from the 1950s, when the team won five European Cups in succession. The white of Real Madrid—Royal Madrid—was assigned after receiving a blessing from King Alfonso XIII in 1920. Seen as the team of a centralized Castilian state hostile to regions such as Catalonia and the Basque Country, the club was anathema to many on the left. Games against the Franco's favourite team thus held extra incentive for those visiting from the Basque and Catalan regions especially during Franco's reign. The streets around the stadium are quiet and empty now. We drive past Opium, the most exclusive disco in Madrid. It has only just closed its doors and the pavement is full of "boys with money and girls looking for boys with money," as Vicente says. The boys have long hair to their shoulders and open shirts showing hairless chests, while the girls also have shoulder-long hair and short skirts. It's not unusual to see many of the *futbolistas* of Real Madrid here on a weekend after a game, Vicente says. He also tells me that there are high-end brothels around here and his night driving job is often to bring clients to such places in Salamanca.

"They have us on commission, so we bring them to certain places," he says, implying that the clubs and brothels look after the taxi drivers. A few weeks ago Vicente brought one client to a local brothel or *casa de lujo* that he has an arrangement with. Because the client stayed in the brothel for four hours, where clients can be charged up to €360 an hour, Vicente received a commission of €280 just for dropping him at the door and picking him up when he was done.

Apart from the spill of people outside the club, the streets of Salamanca are quiet; we see clipped hedges, mansions and boutiques, though not much life. Vicente drives us along Calle de Serrano, "the golden mile," he calls it—the richest stretch in the city. The street is lined with parked Mercedes and BMWs and Gucci and D&G stores. At the end is the US Embassy, where, even at this hour, there are three police vans in front monitoring the darkness: "When there's a dignitary staying they'll put a tank out front," Vicente says with a straight face.

He tells me stories about the city, some from other taxi drivers who have driven here at night for generations, as we pass the giant towers on the edge of the motorway looping out towards the east. "My dad brought two people out here near the end of his career," Vicente says. "That's the problem with taxis, people always sit behind you and you can't see what they're doing. They were well dressed and he didn't think anything until near the end of the fare. The lady stuck a knife against his neck and the man put a gun to his head. They stole his money and his taxi. He was stranded."

"What did he do?" I ask.

"He caught a cab home, of course. They let him pay later," he adds with a smile. "Where to next?" he asks as we pass the high walls of government apartment blocks.

"How about Cañada Real Galiana?" I suggest as an antidote to the opulence of Salamanca.

He doesn't reply for a moment, so I repeat it again. He holds his hand up for me to wait and he gets on his radio. Vicente has never been through the slum and he's nervous.

"This is the most dangerous part of Madrid, especially in a taxi," he says. "We need help if we want to go there."

He gets on his radio to other taxi drivers to plot the safest course through the middle of this shantytown congregation of more than 30,000 people. Vicente has an app on his phone, Cello, which is like a two-way radio frequency he and his taxi driver friends are all tuned into. Vicente puts out our request and the taxi collective give their advice: don't go, go somewhere else, lock your doors. We finally hear from Pepe who lives near the edge of the slum; he suggests a road we can take straight through the middle and we "should" be fine as long as we turn left at the school before entering the "shooting gallery" where most of the drug transactions take place. As Vicente talks to other drivers on the app, I appreciate the community they have when they work together like this. This is what they don't want Uber to replace.

Despite its warranted reputation for drugs and danger, Cañada Real, the biggest slum in the city, is also where many migrants, from Morocco and Latin America, as well as Spanish citizens, end up as a last resort. Many families come out here and just build a shack on the edge of the slum from whatever materials they can find—wood, plastic, old cinder blocks and shreds of carpet—in order to have some sort of home and semi-permanent shelter.

As we head out into the *periferias* he tells me about the *kundas*—these are the taxis the drug dealers and addicts use to get to the heavier *barrios*. "Drug addicts drive them," he says. "Many places you can't get in unless you're known, so a junkie will drive another in to score heroin or coke,"

"How do they pay for it?" I ask.

"They don't," Vicente replies. "They give them a cut. So they might give them some of coke for the return trip. It's very common."

I ask how a *kunda* can be spotted, "It's the *polvo*—dust on the wheels," the dirt from the unpaved roads of the slum.

There are two main reasons the slum is famous, apart from the drugs. The city's largest rubbish tip and refuse incinerating centre is right in the middle of Cañada Real, so this is where up to 4,000 of the city's rubbish trucks trundle back and forth from every day. It's also where many of the *barrio*'s kids will hang around.

"They throw rocks at any trucks or cars that don't belong. Sometimes they set up a road block or deflate your tyres so you have to pay a *multa* to get out," Vicente adds.

"When people normally ask to go to Cañada Real, what do you say?" I ask.

"No," he replies.

"I take people to the edges sometimes; a prostitute did a house call out here a while back. She was squirming around in the back seat putting on all her leather gear while we drove. A few weeks ago I brought out this lady, maybe fifty or sixty years old, she was well dressed and polite, and she just wanted to be dropped at the roundabout so she could score heroin."

As we drive we see a *kunda* labouring in the slow lane. It is a beaten up maroon Toyota with dusty tyres, as Vicente said. The car is full of dishevelled looking men in coats and hats wiping their noses with their hands and shaking their shoulders up and down in anticipation.

"I'm not sure, though I've been told that a driver will get half a gram of coke for the journey," says Vicente.

We loop to the right from the road towards Rivas-Vaciamadrid and quickly it is dark and quiet. Unintentionally I'm leaving mental breadcrumbs again—a deserted petrol station, a quiet truck stop, a sign to watch out for deer crossing the road and a house with a small mountain of toilet seats and cracked bowls in the front of it. There are only intermittent streetlights out here and there is more real, natural darkness than anywhere else I've been so far tonight.

The main reason for the slum's notoriety is its reputation as Madrid's main outdoor drugs supermarket. It is estimated by police that 90 per cent of the city's illegal drug supply is channelled through the dusty streets of Cañada Real. Most of the deals take place along a one-kilometre-long open-air "shooting gallery" within the township. Even now I see people slumped in the back of their cars, but it's impossible to know whether they're riding a high or just sleeping till dawn. During the day the main market area can have up to fifty cars lined on either side of the track with their occupants waiting to score.

There are also many people here who have no choice and aren't involved in the illegal trades of the *barrio*: Moroccans, Roma people and Spaniards who have reached the end of the line and have nowhere else to go without taking their families to live on the streets. There are schools here now, shops, a church, a doctor and a dentist as well as people who are struggling and striving for a normal life on the edges of the "shooting gallery".

Cañada Real is built along an old sheep herding path which leads into the city, and, while this slum that extends out from a dry riverbed is on public land, all the houses we see in the dim yellow light, the big back fences, the corrugated iron walls and tarpaulin roofs are illegal.

Vicente's friend and fellow taxi driver, Pepe, reminds us of our route over the radio, "Make sure you turn left once you get to the school, because after that it's the worst area … for the drug dealers… You won't get out of there," he says through the crackling radio. Vicente locks the doors and we continue inside.

There are supposedly 30,000 people who live here and a few years ago up to 10,000 addicts would travel the sixteen kilometres south-east of the city centre on the 339 bus or share a ride in a *kunda* to score cocaine or heroin from the dealers. A car flicks its lights on behind us and begins following at a not too discreet distance—we are in the slum now and too far along the rutted, muddy track to attempt any sort of retreat.

"Put your notepad away!" Vicente orders me as we approach a group of *gitanos* sitting by the bumpy road. They're scouts, and no doubt the arrival of a taxi has been passed down the line—hopefully just as a curiosity. The light here is different. In the city the streetlights are laid out at regular intervals and spray out a soft orange glow from the innovative LED globes. Here there are intermittent cheap yellow bulbs hanging on the corners of the street. Everything seems damp and full of puddles of darkness. I can see the houses squashed next to each other like Monopoly pieces snaking up into the distance from the dirt track to the left of the main thoroughfare. Up ahead of the taxi the silhouette of three men walking on the road with a dog at their side appears. I notice the flicker of a TV screen behind a ripped curtain as we drive past and the glow of Madrid on the far horizon. Much of the light here comes from fires lit in oil drums and from piles of refuse. There is a sense of danger here, though I don't know if it's imagined because I know reputation of the place, or from the sight of Vicente's white knuckles as he drives.

As he drives and I observe, there are many signs of normal life: a pink toddler's bike up against a fence, curtains with cartoon heroes drawn across the fly screen of a child's room, cats peacefully sleeping in doorways in a knot of mother and kittens. I look down the lanes and it is different; garbage is piled high against the shanty walls, old car parts lie rusting along in front of houses and more *gitanos* sit on picnic chairs at the junctions in the darkness illuminated only by the glow of their cigarettes.

I see a gym, another group of walking *gitanos* and up ahead the junction of the *plaza* and the drug market. This is not a place we can enter at night, in a taxi or without prior approval. We turn left at the school— Cañada Real Mario Benedetti, as Pepe instructed, and for the first time in minutes Vicente breathes out and releases his grip on the wheel.

"It's the first time I've been here," he says. "And the last." I laugh at the release of anxiety, though he's not quite ready to relax from the encounter.

"A taxi means money out here," he says, highlighting how conspicuous we are, even at night.

I furiously scribble observations in my notepad, now that it is safe to reveal it again, though I notice that when I don't have the security of a notepad or recording device to capture an experience, my senses are much more sharply tuned: I notice the difference in the streetlights here, the smell of wood smoke and diesel, the ominous lanes which spoke off from the main artery and the spikes on the tops of the fences which maybe I wouldn't see otherwise.

After we turn at the school and make our way back to the main road, there is a collective sigh of relief from the taxi drivers over the radio, who are all glad that Vicente made it through. In this changing transport era, where the demand for taxis will be challenged by Uber or some other ride sharing enterprise, these drivers seem to stick together, whether on advice on how to get a travel writer through a slum, or a tip for another fare during peak hour.

Back on the main road another driver tells us over the radio that we're lucky we got through today. He went through Cañada Real the other day and a group of *gitanos* closed access to the *barrio*. There was a fight with the Moroccans over territory and cables that the groups steal from building sites during the night. They didn't want witnesses, or people in the middle, so everyone was turned away until it was resolved.

"You don't know how dangerous what you just did could have been," he adds.

On the way back we drive past Valdemingómez, where the "glorieta de drogas" is. It's a roundabout not far from Cañada Real, where you can only enter if you have a pass, normally issued by the police, as beyond the roundabout is a lawless area of drugs and dealers where our safety can't be guaranteed.

Tonight the *glorieta* is quiet, maybe we're too late, or too early; we can only see a handful of junkies slouched in the bushes as we do three circuits and then shoot off back to Madrid.

We pass a line of ten or twelve rubbish trucks heading towards the city from the slum and another *kunda* heading back into the dark guts of the Cañada Real.

"Where do they start?" I ask of the drug taxis.

It seems as good a route as any back into the city, so Vicente drives me via Parque del Oeste, where we see a group of transvestites propositioning men in cars, to the district of Embajadores where the *kundas* begin their service. He doesn't know why it begins here in this relatively prosperous part of the city, though there they are, the beaten up cars with white, dusty wheels next to the Metro station waiting for customers to take to Cañada Real to score.

It is quite unreal. Fifteen minutes after being in the centre of the slum we are now driving through some of the fanciest neighbourhoods in Madrid as we head towards the centre past the Paseo del Prado, which is slowly coming to life again, and the bustle around Atocha where the trains are about to begin running.

Our time is nearly up. My bill approaches €80, though I'm happy with the perspective that Vicente has given me of the night-time taxi driver's life.

"My largest fare was all the way to Galicia," he says, referring to the province in the north of Spain where the Camino de Santiago pilgrim route finishes. "A man was in a rush for work, so his company paid me €600 Euros for 600 kilometres."

Our last stop before he drops me off and finishes his shift is at one of the taxi drivers' petrol stations and clubhouses. The petrol pumps and the car park are full. All these drivers are finishing their night shift and getting ready to go to bed. Vicente puts €50 worth into his car, the petrol is 25 cents a litre cheaper than on the street. He yawns for the first time tonight and stretches his back on the edge of his taxi. It's as if he has released his grip on the night and he's ready to sleep through the day, before he drives again tonight. With the darkness beginning to ebb, it is that strange hour of the day where the night's tendrils are not entirely gone, yet the energy of the daylight hasn't yet arrived. Vicente is going home, so he drops me back in the centre, at the edge of Chueca, on Calle de Hortaleza, and close to where I was only a few hours ago.

As the sky begins to shift colours and the layers of black begin to peel ever so slightly, the district has a crustier feeling. The sense of possibility and the alertness of the night seem lost. The senses are dulled until the sun comes up. This is the time to disappear if you have been up for the duration of the night. Daylight doesn't have the same shadows and mysteries, and this bleak and flat hour is depressing. Dawn is the only time I'm cold in Madrid; the stone walls retain no heat and the pavement is clear and slick. This is the hour when a fever reaches breaking point, or when a hangover begins to pulse in the veins at the side of your temple. I'm not done yet, though, and I continue walking. Up ahead I see a red carpet on the cobblestones. I see one open door at the end of the street and I decide to enter it to see what's inside.

6am: Iglesia

I have been one acquainted with the night ... I have outwalked the furthest city light.
Robert Frost, "Acquainted with the Night", 1928

I sit next to the confessional box of Padre Angel waiting as he directs the volunteers to put the crib outside the new toilets and next to the altar.

"Someone left a baby in the rubbish out here last week," he says, pointing to the street behind him. "Our doors are always open, so if people know we now have a *cuna*—a crib—hopefully it won't happen like that again."

I am with Padre Angel in the Iglesia de San Antón in Chueca, a downtown church which is doing something that many Christian places of worship throughout the world seem to have given up doing; they are leaving their doors open, 24 hours a day, to provide care and hope for those people in Madrid who really need it. Through the open doors Padre Angel and I see the last moments of darkness evaporating outside. The day has not yet begun, but the padre waits for the people who will arrive with the light. He is a Catholic priest, though he looks more like a grizzled newspaper editor; he wears a wrinkled suit, he has gold rings on his fingers and his red tie is loosened around his neck. Despite his age, in his seventies I imagine, it is difficult to see the tiredness behind his drive.

Despite the privileged position of the Catholic Church in Spain, where during Franco's rule external manifestations of other non-Catholic forms of worship were banned (something which was not rectified in the Constitution until 1978), Padre Angel's church does not seem to rest on the laurels of the past, even though 90 per cent of the population are baptized as Roman Catholic in Spain.

The Iglesia de San Antón looks grandly ornate on first inspection, with various statues of Mary and Jesus, a gigantic golden organ, a shrine to St Valentine, a large altar backed by the crucifix and majestic light filtering down from the dome of the church. As I look closer, I see that the walls are peeling, the fresco on the ceiling is worn, the statues are chipped and

St Anthony, patron saint of animals, with a pig, Iglesia San Antón, Chueca (Antonio Velez/ Wikimedia Commons)

the organ seems to be an electronic imitation. I like this. I am suspicious of the wealth and extravagance churches display in the face of those who need them, so these rough edges endear me to the padre and his mission. They've only been open for four months and Padre Angel took his prompt from Pope Francis who said that "Churches should have their doors open in all parts for those who are looking for God and can't find him." He tells me that he took the pope's words to heart and decided to open this place all night, every night, to help people "find a little peace," he says with a slight grin. In the place of golden candle holders, silver goblets and grand stained glass windows, the padre uses the church's funds to custom fit facilities for the needy with toilets, sinks and a baby changing facility, to offer free Wi-Fi for people to maintain connections with the outside world, to put comfortable cushions on the benches and to make food and drink available for those in need. There is also a food vending machine at the front of the church. Visitors put money in and it will give credit to a person in need to buy food: €3 for eggs, €5 for meat, €1 for pasta or a tin of sardines.

"People aren't as giving these days," he declares, alluding to the general malaise in Madrid that has necessitated his unique church services. "The people who come here are desperate—we listen, rather than just preach," he says as an implicit challenge to the way many churches operate.

I notice pillows laid out on the hard wooden pews, "It's if someone needs to have a rest."

"We help the people who don't exist," he says of those who are on the edge of society here. "We also bless animals," he adds as a scruffy black dog bounds along the aisles with its owner.

This is possibly what the church is most renowned for in Madrid. St Anthony, the patron of this church, also used to bless animals, Padre Angel tells me, so once a year, on 17 January, they do the same. People will line up around the corner of the long street in order to get a blessing for their companion.

"For many people their dog, or their cat, is their life. If they have no family it can be all they have," he says as the black dog jumps up on the sacerdotal table waiting for a pat. "That's why we bless people's animals: dogs, turtles, snakes, parrots, even fish," he adds with pride.

"What are they looking for from the blessing?" I ask.

"The same as what most people want, a longer life and prosperity," answers Padre Angel.

There is a buzz of energy around this place and a sense of excitement about the future, something rare in a church, I would guess.

"What are your plans?" I ask him.

He pauses to think for a moment, "Our plans are to continue to care for people." It seems a simple goal, though much less simple in practice as I observe from all the movement even at this hour.

"People who come here feel forgotten—they've come out of prison, they live on the street, they have no roof and no food," he says as I notice the way in which the people in his church can let their guard down and sit with their eyes closed, or sip a drink with a relative feeling of security, even if only for a fleeting moment.

I notice a defibrillator on the wall, one of their recent purchases, and I have to ask, "Have you used it?"

He smiles, "No, not yet. With all this work, though, maybe they'll use it on me!"

There are TV screens here with sermons from the Vatican and community information for those who live in the area. There is also a wall of plugs for charging phones and a table with tea, coffee, pastries and juice for whoever wants to enter the church. In the corner I notice dry dog food in a bowl by the door, confirming that this place really is open to all. A sign on the door announces that inside the doors of the church it is permitted to drink your fill of cold water, change your baby, repair your heart (literally or spiritually) and take photos.

It is true that this church is trying to open its arms to outsiders and to create a stronger Catholic bond with the community, though it is done in one of the most respectful and open ways. This wasn't always so. While much of the Iberian Peninsula was known as al-Andalus, the Islamic state created by Muslims who crossed over from North Africa through Jabal Tariq or Gibraltar in 711, there was almost constant Christian resistance to this rule as the 770-year *Reconquista* or Christian struggle to seize back the territory began in the mountainous north of Spain in 722. During this period the Muslim rulers in the south, in the caliphate of Córdoba, presided over one of the most enlightened places in Western Europe, with 500,000 citizens living among palaces, gardens, libraries and a centre for learning and translation. During the period to 1031 there was coexistence and acceptance between the Muslims, Christians and Jews within the caliphate, though this wouldn't last. As Christians from the north began to converge on the south, led by warrior chiefs such as Sancho the Fat and Wilfred the Hairy, Toledo was captured in 1085, giving an enormous boost to the morale of the Christian forces. Eventually power shifted towards these Christian forces and by 1264 Granada was the only Muslim city left in Spain. Granada eventually fell in 1492, though not before the Jewish population was also ordered to leave Spain or be killed by the Inquisitors. The re-conquest paved the way for King Fernando II and Queen Isabella I, the first of the Catholic monarchs, to establish the Inquisition in 1478 in order to create a religiously unified Spain through any means necessary. The Catholic monarchs, supported by Cardinal Francisco Jiménez de Cisneros, who burned every Islamic book he could find, ordered that all Muslims either be baptized as Catholics or go into exile. Hence the population of *moriscos*, or converted Muslims, was created in Spain, which became a wholly Catholic country (in name at least) around the time that Madrid was recognized as the capital.

Even from a modern perspective, the open stance of Padre Angel's church is at odds with the closed view of the ruling clergy. When José Luis Rodríguez Zapatero's Socialist Party formed a government in Spain in 2004 it paved the way for the legalization of same sex marriage, abortion and divorce (creating a remarkably open Catholic country). During Zapatero's term in office from 2004 to 2011, however, the Archbishop of Madrid, Cardinal Antonio Rouco Varela, declared that Spain was becoming a modern "Sodom and Gomorrah", and many demonstrations to "defend family values" were staged in the city at the time to resist the reforms.

I am not religious in the slightest, but there is something immensely impressive about the openness of the Iglesia de San Antón as an example of what a modern church can do without being shackled by the expectations of the past.

Padre Angel excuses himself, as he must prepare as a film crew will be coming soon to further spread the word of his church. I sit in a row at the back for a moment, alone, as the last fibres of the night disappear through the open door. I wander through the church and see the shrines to St Valentine and to Santa Lucia, the patron of the blind, and while it all looks worn, it is obvious that the church's funds, which all come from donations, are put to good use. There is a sign on the side wall which reads: "Un poco de misercordia cambia el mundo, lo hace menos frio y mas justo." "A little mercy can change the world, to make it less cold and more just."

As I sit a few people wander inside. One man who looks as if he slept rough last night makes for the toilets, another lady pours herself a coffee, and a few tourists walk inside to soak in the silence and take discreet photos before it gets busy.

While Padre Angel chats to the film crew I talk to two volunteers who have been here all night. José and Pedro prepare the church for the day as we talk, sweeping the entrance, turning the lights on at the altar and switching the bright lights at the entrance off.

José is dressed in a shirt and pink tie. Despite the early hour he still looks fresh and he brings me a cup of freshly brewed coffee as we chat. He is out of work at the moment and he says the church helped him when things were very difficult for him and his family, so now he gives up his nights, from 2am until 8am for the church until something else comes along. His companion, Pedro, is homeless and his volunteering means that he is working for a good cause and he has shelter during the night.

"Con la frialdad de las puertas cerradas" ("from the coldness of closed doors") comes Padre Angel's motivation for this place with its doors open. The church is getting busier as those who have endured the night arrive for sustenance.

I say goodbye to Padre Angel and his helpers as the sound of someone practising on the organ above us fills the space. If night signifies death and fear, then this place is certainly keeping them at bay—it is hopeful and friendly, and even in the dark corners people, and their problems, are welcome.

"Feliz es quien ama y se deja amar," Padre Angel says—happy is the one who loves and is loved—as a parting thought on the mission of his church.

The streets are just beginning to open their eyes and emerge from their blankets. There is no colour in the city yet, except grey, though the brief sleep of Madrid is over. The first day workers stride into Metro stations or sip coffee while perched on stools of cafés that have just rolled up their security doors. This is a small window where the world of the night intersects with the world of the day. Night workers in their high visibility uniforms ascend the stairs of the Metro as men and women in suits stride along the street to begin their working day.

Pedro and José stand at the open doors as I leave. They watch Madrid come to life and wait for the first people to come in for a coffee or some peace. The last thing I see of the church is the plaque at the entrance: "Leave what you can and take what you need". I see the donations piled by the door and the people who slot their spare euros into the vending machine.

The Iglesia de San Antón is not alone in its fight to help the needy in Madrid. Before I finish my nightwalking Padre Angel has suggested that I pay a visit to the *comedor* up the street. Pedro draws me a map and I follow it up towards the Iglesia Metro stop to one of the inner city's homeless shelters to see how many of the people who come to Padre Angel's church spend the night and survive the day.

The *comedor*, or canteen, is a St Vincent de Paul shelter on a busy street up from the church. The gate is closed, though already there are four people lining up, waiting to be admitted. Just like the airport, there's no real difference in appearance between the people queuing and those walking past on their way to work or school. Despite the desperation of those in line, they blend into the street. They have acquired a type of camouflage, just like those who live at the airport. One of the men in the queue puffs on a bent cigarette and holds a bible close to his chest with his other hand; he grasps the book tightly, as if it is a lifebuoy and the only thing that kept him afloat through the long night now behind him. Others waiting in the line carry blankets and plastic bags with toothbrushes, spare socks and school books inside.

A security guard in a brown uniform and sporting a flat top admits us inside the large stone building. He's irritable and he barks at me to sit down and wait my turn as I arrive. There are others in here now as well; it is like a hospital waiting room, where homeless people and those who need some help come to be put on the social services' register. Old ladies wearing tracksuits and crumpled looking men who still bother to slick their hair back and wear collared shirts sit around me waiting their turn. A group of three men barge through the doors demanding to go upstairs to eat; they have strange shaved heads and crude tattoos on their necks and their Spanish has a chewed sounding accent I don't recognize. The guard blocks their path and demands that they sit down, or they'll never be welcome again. I understand now why the guard was so short with me as I asked questions: this is a volatile place and the people are understandably desperate, though without his order it would be chaos. The men nod reluctantly to the guard and sit in front of the television, which is playing a re-run of a Bear Grylls show where he is teaching people how to survive in extreme and unlikely situations. It seems slightly absurd to me—as the skills and resilience the people in this room must have to survive on the streets every night in Madrid are surely more worthy than the urine-drinking, bug-eating tips proffered by the expert survivalist on the screen above us.

Once I meet the social workers I explain who I am and they take me to meet the matron of the *comedor*, Josefa, the nun who is in charge of the facility. She has salt and pepper hair and bright green eyes behind her glasses. She's happy that I'm interested in what they're doing and she gladly walks with me through the building. "Our main aim is to try and integrate people into the system, to give them a hand to help themselves achieve what they need, whether that's a meal, identity papers or a place for their family to stay the night," she says as we climb the stairs. Outside I see the church across the quadrangle and a group of young kids playing football on the stones. Josefa explains what it is they do for the people who sleep rough, who are between jobs or homes or who might be on the edge of something much more dangerous.

"We have a room for people during the day, with TV, Internet, a library and we have a programme to help immigrants settle in Madrid," she says.

I ask what they do for people who have nowhere to go during the night and she points to a wing of the building where they have fifteen beds; "these are for families and emergency situations." Often these emergencies can last for up to three months if children or violent situations are involved.

As the next step they help people into *pisos*, apartments, where they can get on their feet with a sense of independence. "Our aim is help people see that they can have a future."

We walk up another flight of stairs to the *comedor* itself, the dining room that fits 120 people for each of the three sittings for meals here every day. Cooks are bringing loaves of still steaming bread from the ovens, baking cakes, slicing beef and chicken and chopping vegetables in preparation for the first service.

"We feed nearly 400 people a day here, they all get a card and it permits them to come in once a day for a meal," Josefa says.

Even with this sort of charity they are still very aware of dietary needs, and because of the large Muslim population they are very careful when serving pork and keeping it separate.

With such a large influx of people there are always problems, Josefa admits. Sometimes individuals create trouble if they are coming off drugs, though normally, "people are very grateful for what we provide," she adds, "we give our time, we listen to them and we help where we can."

The aim is to give people hope, to help give people a leg up in order to create a future for themselves, whether looking for a job, a place to sleep or papers to allow them to stay in Spain legally. There's also a hairdresser, a library, a nurse, an employment exchange, a geriatrics department and a place for printing and fixing CVs to give access to some of the more normal aspects of life.

As we pass by I see little kids playing on the stairs while we walk and talk. "There's much solidarity between the people of Madrid," Josefa says.

This is an important place as it does help people survive the nights, and it also gives them hope that they can make it through the next one as well and do something positive in the process. Josefa tells me that they even have Spanish classes because something as simple and vital as language is often what many migrants are lacking when they arrive in the city. "We're not just a *comedor*, we try to integrate people into the system."

We arrive back at the waiting room on the first floor. It is full of people listening to music on their earphones, reading folded newspapers and watching the television. Young women and old men greet Josefa warmly as she takes me to the door. She smiles and touches the waiting people on the shoulders as she passes. I say goodbye to Josefa as the tide of people entering increases before the first meal sitting.

After all the darkness and the struggle I have witnessed, the work that Padre Angel and Josefa do to help people in need of a little light and a little help shows me, I think, what *solidaridad* between the people in Madrid means.

I exit back out onto the street and I am nearly done with my exploration. I am dizzy, though I want to finish how I started—walking.

7am: Final walk

The Night is my other day. The most prodigious half of my life.
Hélène Cixous, "Writing Blind", 1998

My feet are heavy now. I trip and stumble towards the Metro and squeeze into the carriage as it takes me towards my last stop. My eyes close unintentionally as we bounce around the underground curves. I open them with a start as the automated voice tells me that my stop is approaching. Summoning the last bit of alertness I have left, I get out at Ciudad Universitaria, ready for my last walk.

Roberto Bolaño writes in his novel *2666* that nightwalkers are two types of people, "those running out of time and those with time to burn". Now, finally, I know that I am running out of time. The sky is turning a whiteish blue and the night has disappeared except for the last hologram of the moon and a few stars. I have one final thing I want to do; I want to go back to the beginning, and I want to walk there.

The origins of Madrid are hazy. Some say it was originally founded by the Romans, others by the Phoenicians. My aim for the last walk is to finish at the spot where it is rumoured that modern Madrid began. Some of the best stories of this city, of its past and its present, seem to stem from myths and tales, so I think it's appropriate to finish on what may have been the first.

The streets are busy again after those few quiet hours where the temperature cools and the city closes its eyes ever so briefly to recharge. I walk past a blind lady navigating the street with her stick. The night is mostly over in Madrid now, though it strikes me that it wouldn't matter to her as it does to me; the fear of the dark, the avoidance of the unknown is something she wouldn't face as I do. For her it would be a constant struggle, or an altered sense of reality, rather than a once a day temporal occurrence. Darkness does enhance the sensory experience of place, as I have realized during my night in Madrid. Imagine being in darkness all the time and constructing your experience of place using the other senses. It would be a strange and quite illuminating thing to experience a city with a blind person.

Travel and blindness is nothing new. James Holman travelled the world in the nineteenth century as a blind adventurer, charting the Australian outback, escaping captivity in Siberia and hunting rogue elephants in Sri Lanka without ever "seeing" any of it in a conventional sense. The very notion of having sight and being able to rely on it to travel does change the way we interpret place and what we tune into. The Algerian-born writer and philosopher Hélène Cixous writes that her sight impairs her ability to see beyond the raw vision of the world: "I want to see what is secret. What is hidden amongst the visible." I think that nightwalking goes some way to allowing this to occur; it presents different images, new stories and other people. "I want to see the skin of the light," Cixous continues, and I wonder whether that's exactly what the night is, the skin of the day, covering and concealing things within it.

From the stairs of the Metro I walk across the square to a statue of a muscled young man on a horse bending down to take a lit torch from an old, prostrate man on the ground: *Los portadores de la antorcha*, "The Torch Bearers", by the American sculptor Anna Hyatt Huntington. I look at this exquisite piece, now framed by more modern student graffiti, and I imagine it symbolizes the journey of the student and the power of education, though more powerfully for me I think it evokes the importance of transition, something at which Madrid seems to be very adept. One only has to look as far as the influence of former lecturer Pablo Iglesias and his party Podemos to understand this taste for change.

Before I walk to the river I stop to look at the buildings to see whether there are still scars from the civil war that consumed the university campus in the 1930s. Being a university lecturer in my other life, I'm familiar with daily life on campus, though as I walk towards the looming columns of the Faculty of Medicine while students wearing Pink Floyd t-shirts juggle books and professors lugging leather satchels pass me, I can't fathom how strange it would have been in 1936 when the university sent letters out to the students warning that the term would be delayed "until further notice" because of the civil war which was spiralling towards their classrooms. Many would never set foot on the campus again.

Right here in this square was where the first wave of the savage fighting between republicans and nationalists took place. The nationalists, led by Franco's Army of Africa, or the "Bridegrooms of Death" as they were also known, were looking for a way into the city

Los portadores de la antorcha (Carlos Delgado; CC-BY-SA)

streets after slogging through the unpopulated Casa de Campo for a week, fighting the republicans on the hills and in the river beds of this former hunting reserve in the west of the city. Once they arrived at the university, where a place of learning was to be turned into a death trap, they decided that the route across the Manzanares river at the Puente de los Franceses next to the campus was the place to attack, as it would allow them to create a supply chain from their forces in the Casa de Campo towards their goal in the city proper. More than 6,000 nationalist soldiers flooded towards the university in three columns. Hungarian volunteer troops defended the French-built Casa de Velázquez on the campus, and died to the last man, while international *brigadistas* helped stop more nationalists in the square, despite their bombarding of the Medicine and Pharmacy Faculties. One volunteer from the International Brigades said that the fighting was so fierce in the university that blood ran down the stairs. The volunteers, many famous writers and intellectuals among them, would pile books against the open windows to prevent sniper hits while they were reinforcing the rooms. They used the thickest books they could find and discovered that the bullets would generally penetrate to about page 350. After the initial intensity of the fighting it became a war of attrition and eventually the focus of the battle moved elsewhere in the city. It was one of the great victories for the republicans and it played an important role in delaying the taking of Madrid.

As I walk closer to the Faculty of Medicine I decide to go inside the building. Students are going to the library, others downstairs to what I think is the cafeteria. It's the first time that I feel like I'm trespassing. While I'm inside the building there is a change in the sky as it fades to a tint of darkest blue; the night is over. The *madrugada*—dawn—has arrived. Once I am outside I see the gouged pockmarks on the side of the building and its supporting columns. They're now filled in with cement, though the origins of these scars are unmistakable. Even after all these years, there are still stark reminders of the civil war here and how it affected every aspect of the *Madrileños*' lives. Students chat and balance stacks of books as they filter along the pavement between buildings. To think that right here, less than seventy years ago, there were soldiers barrelling through the tutorial rooms, charging one another on stairwells and shooting each other in libraries. It seems absurd.

From the campus I walk along the avenue, now teeming with university students heading to their first class of the day, towards the library and to the Arco de la Victoria.

My nightwalking as a *trasnochador*—one who stays up all night—has allowed me to see through a different temporal lens while appreciating a new way of "apprehending our urban environment", as Merlin Coverley writes. It has enabled me to explore the city beyond the banal and monotonous everyday experience. I think that this has revealed that in reality there is more light during the night than we realize in both a literal and figurative sense.

The smell of pinesap is in the air; the flags in the distance are still flapping, though the air is becoming stiller. Above me is the Faro de Moncloa, the space age viewing platform that looks out to the mountains and the southern plains.

I cross the now busy lines of traffic that skirt past the edges of the Arco de la Victoria, the 49-metre arch with a chariot and rider on top. The structure somewhat resembles the Arc de Triomphe in Paris, though it does not celebrate the sort of victory that is relished in today's Madrid. The vaulting grey arch was built at the request of Franco in 1956 to commemorate his victory in taking the city in 1939. I find it strange that it still remains as a symbol of the Franco years when so many other statues and plaques have been removed or beheaded. It also seems a little strange that something like this is so visible, even if it is not often spoken about, and that there are very few official avenues for people to commemorate the loss of life within the war and the battles that gripped the city's streets for more than three years.

There are mattresses set up in one of the enormous structure's alcoves to provide night-time shelter for the homeless—at least someone is getting good use from the structure. The Arco looks much older than it is, possible due to the thousands of cars and trucks which belch exhaust fumes all over the monument day and night.

From the Arco I pass the gigantic Ejército del Aire building, the air force headquarters¬. With ornate towers at its the corners and thousands of rooms, it looks like an Austrian palace. From there I cut through the Parque del Oeste. The woods are thick here. It seems like a winter garden full of heavy firs, spongy grass and a snaking stream below me. Despite its beauty, it is one site I'm now glad to see in the first smudges of daylight.

The Arco de la Victoria (César Astudillo/Wikimedia Commons)

During the night it is another prostitute and drug hot spot and during the civil war there were more than 200 mines planted in the rolling hills that fold down towards the river. Many soldiers and civilians would have used the cover of darkness here in the park to travel to their homes or between the fronts despite the danger. It is said that in the aftermath of the war this ornamental park resembled the Western Front because of the carnage and incessant shelling that took place here and because of the crude trenches that were cut into the scorched hills. Even in the early Franco years this park was a place of horror, as many of the rebels and republican sympathizers were killed and their bodies dumped in the leaf litter under the trees.

Now it is lovely, the air is cool, there are birds in the branches above and the only person I see is a kid on an oversized skateboard slaloming to the bottom of the hill. It seems like a winter paradise in the first moments of the day. This park has a different feel to it from the Retiro; it seems more secluded and private. I watch the wall of apartments on the edge of the park above me and keep them on my left as I skip down past the swing sets and clipped hedges to a graffiti-decorated crossing over the train tracks. I'm close now and I cross back into the traffic, on the edge of the Príncipe Pío shopping complex, to the river that has defined much of the development, conflict and imagination of the city of Madrid for centuries.

Seeing the Río Manzanares doesn't have quite the impact I expected. I doubt I could even clean my socks properly in the river if I wanted to. The water is ankle deep at best; little islets break the streams up, so it looks more like a funnel of water shooting out from the gutter of an old man washing his Alfa Romeo on a Sunday morning upstream. Victor Hugo was once dining in the city and it is said that he ordered a glass of water with his meal, though rather than drinking the glass he left it half empty and told the waiter to tip the rest back in the Manzanares, as it evidently needed it more than he did.

Elizabeth Nash noted of the famous river: "The Manzanares is not the Seine, or the Thames or the Tiber. Rather, it is a line of spit, wrote the 17th-century satirist Francisco de Quevedo, where frogs and mosquitoes die of thirst. Alexandre Dumas, who planned to write about the Manzanares, 'couldn't find it'." When the handsome Segovia Bridge was built in 1583, Lope de Vega, Spain's Shakespeare, advised the authorities to sell it, or buy a river.

Like many things I've seen, though, which don't fit the preconceived image I had of them, this quirky "line of spit" defines the city nonetheless. It has withheld armies and generals, it has avoided the re-routing and damming of bigger rivers and it still maintains a trickle despite global warming and urban development. It is a stubborn survivor and a symbol of the city's resilience. I turn back away from the river and huff up the hill past the shopping mall where early morning junkies sip their beers on the steps of the Metro and shop workers filter inside. I'm walking purely on adrenaline now. I can feel things getting closer. An ending is coming. My steps quicken. I'm no longer a stroller. I want to find that "x" or that finish line, even if it is imagined, to put a full stop on my night walk.

The Templo de Debod (M. Peinado/Wikimedia Commons)

I take wrong turns and enter dead ends; even though I've been at this for more than twelve hours I still get lost and take the long way to get where I'm going. For a *flâneur*, I think it's a blessing. When we script things too much and try to plan for every contingency, travel, whether walking around Madrid by night or driving across Australia, loses some of its magic. Stephen Muecke writes about the power of embracing chance encounters in his book on Madagascar as he commits to sitting and watching his surroundings like a surfer in the ocean, "waiting for the feeling of the swell rising under us and propelling us forward, demanding our skill and knowledge of the wave". By paying attention to what is going on around him he lets the place, in this case Madagascar, speak to him rather than allowing his own itinerary to conceal things he would have otherwise missed. After my night in Madrid I understand how important it is to embrace the organic unfolding of a story such as this.

My path takes me through another park and up past the Templo de Debod. This strangely cube-like temple that sits by a pool of water like a half-submerged castle was gifted to Madrid by the Egyptian government as a thank you present. The temple was rescued from the flooding waters of Lake Nasser in southern Egypt after the construction of the Aswan Dam and Spanish archaeologists saved the monument from oblivion. The temple dates back to 2200 BC and is said to be the place where the god Horus was born (in Egypt). Just across from the monument is the place where Franco and his forces arrived when they invaded the city in November 1936. In 1968 this spot in the Parque de la Montaña was chosen for the siting of the temple because it was where the barracks stood in which the rebels were executed in the uprising of 1808.

I skip up the wide, stone stairs. Behind the rows of apartments I can see the mountains in the distance, the same ones I saw twelve hours ago, but something has changed. I pass a group of Samur ambulance drivers dressed in yellow and green walking to their vehicles to begin the morning shift. My path takes me close to the Catedral de la Almudena and the Royal Palace, lit up by the streaming sun; I don't want to stop and admire them now. My only interest is to stay on my feet and keep each step from veering into the traffic. I steer past the church of San Nicolás, said by some to be the oldest in the city, and I know that my destination is near. It feels appropriate to end my night where the city began.

The first street laid in Madrid is also another historical bone of contention. Some say it is Calle del Arenal while other historians insist it is Calle de Grafal in La Latina, which dates back to 1190. It is a dark and winding alley fenced in by high apartments and with slick cobble stones which I suppose might be nearly 900 years old. It is nothing remarkable on the surface, though I like the fact that its story and its history remain hidden to the casual observer. To understand its significance you have

The Royal Palace and Catedral de la Almudena seen from the Templo de Debod (Camuñas/ Wikimedia Commons)

to dig a little, just as in most parts of Madrid. I stop at the edge of Madrid's first street for a moment to search for some sort of meaning or resonance in the place where maybe the first stone of the city was laid, though it doesn't come. Madrid is not so easy; I know that now. Just like the Habsburg lisp and the origin of *tapas*, it is a story that is difficult to nail down, though that's okay, I think. There have been many unexpected truths I have discovered in my night in the city, from the sad realities of the people who sleep at the airport terminal to the openness of people like Teresa in Villaverde, who lives in a place I would have avoided before I ventured inside during the hours of darkness.

I'm done. I smile at a lady walking a white poodle; she doesn't smile back, and I keep walking. This isn't a city for empty pleasantries. I stumble to the end of the street and across the road. The open door of the Los Nobles de Castilla café beckons to me and I take a seat at the bar. Inside there are two poker machines and three legs of ham. I order coffee and *churros* and listen to the news on the television above the bar. It's going to be hot today, forty degrees again.

And that's it. The sun is here. Equilibrium has been restored and the night is over. I survived a night unplanned. I remember hearing a saying when I arrived, when you're in Madrid, you are a *Madrileño*. After my night with the city, even for a moment, I think it can be true.

The wind, which began to rustle through the trees twelve hours ago, settles once again. The leaves float and drift back to the gutters. The heat which now pulses from the risen sun is given time to bake into the cold stones and heat up the pavements for the day to come.

Al Alvarez writes that people have lost touch with the night over the last hundred years or so, that we don't really know what true darkness is anymore: "Maybe the foetus in the womb knows it, but even the womb's night is intermittently lit by the ruddy glow that penetrates the mother's body when she takes off her clothes," he writes. I might not know what true darkness is after this walking experiment, though I do feel that the experience of staying awake and engaged with the people and places of the night has given me a much greater understanding of what darkness is in a place like Madrid, one of life and struggle and passion. At the same time it has given me an appreciation of what the night isn't and what I feared it was before I began—it is no longer a time to lock out, to be scared and to wait for daylight to come. I realize now that the night is a time of freedom and opportunity, and this won't be my last night walk in the city. Hemingway said that, "Nobody goes to bed in Madrid until they have killed the night." I think it's the wrong metaphor. The only death is that of one's assumptions. I think you don't know Madrid, just like you don't completely know a lover or a friend, until you've spent the night, awake, together in the city.

Acknowledgements

John Donne wrote many hundreds of years ago that no man is an island and the saying also holds true for this book. *After Dark* could not have happened if it wasn't for the help, guidance and support of many people.

In Spain I am grateful to Jo Wivell, Vicente Sanz, Ramona Varela Garcia, Isabel Varela, Teresa Dorn, Antonio Pablo, Padre Angel, Joy Figueroa and Paco Martinez for helping me during the night. I'm also thankful to the many people I met spontaneously in Madrid after dark, most notably Manolo, Mubarik, Khurum, David and Teresa.

In Australia I am grateful for the assistance of ArtsACT for an initial funding grant, the staff of the journalism department of the University of South Australia for their support and Professor Clayton MacKenzie in particular for encouraging me along the way. I would also like to thank my family for putting up with me, reading drafts and giving me the time to write this book.

In the UK I would like to thank James Ferguson for his support and astute editing.

Lastly I would like to thank the two most important people who made this book a reality, Christian Fiorentino for his enthusiasm and unquestioning help in making all my requests a reality and to Laura, for being behind me every step of the way.

Further reading

Ahmad, Mirza Masroor, *World Crisis and the Pathway to Peace*, London: Islam International Publications, 2012.

Alvarez, Al, *Night: Night Life, Night Language, Sleep, and Dreams*, New York: Norton, 1996.

Augustin, Andreas & Cane, Thomas, *Hotel Ritz Madrid*, Vienna, The Most Famous Hotels in the World, 2008.

Baudelaire, Charles, *Paris Spleen (Le Spleen de Paris)* (1869) (trans. Keith Waldrop), Middletown CT: Wesleyan University Press, 2009.

Beaumont, Matthew, *Nightwalking: A Nocturnal History of London*, London: Verso, 2015.

Beaumont, Matthew & Dart, Gregory (eds), *Restless Cities*, London: Verso, 2010.

Beevor, Antony, The Battle for Spain: *The Spanish Civil War 1936-1939*, London, Penguin, 2006.

Benjamin, Walter, *The Arcades Project*, Cambridge MA: Harvard University Press, 2002.

Bolaño, Roberto, *2666*, London: Picador.

Brenan, Gerald, *The Face of Spain* (1950), London: Serif, 2010.

Botton, Alain de, *The Art of Travel*, London: Hamish Hamilton 2002.

Cabezas, Juan Antonio, *Diccionario de Madrid*, El Avapiés, 1989.

Carandell, Luis, *Madrid*, Madrid: Alianza Cien, 1995.

Chislett, William, *Spain: What Everyone Needs to Know*, Oxford: Oxford University Press, 2013.

Cixous, Hélène, *Stigmata: Escaping Texts*, London: Routledge, 2005.

Conover, Ted, *The Routes of Man: Travels in the Paved World*, New York: Vintage Books, 2010.

Coverley, Merlin, *Psychogeography*, Harpenden: Pocket Essentials, 2010.

De Quincey, Thomas, *Confessions of an English Opium-Eater* (1886), London: Penguin, 2003.

Dickens, Charles, *Night Walks* (1861), London: Penguin, 2010.

Dozy, Reinhart, *Spanish Islam: A History of the Muslims in Spain*, Whitefish MT: Kessinger, 2003.

Ekirch, A. Roger, *At Day's Close: A History of Nighttime Past*, New York: Norton, 2006.

Gibson, Ian, *Federico García* Lorca, London: Faber & Faber, 1990.

Gill, Miranda, *Eccentricity and the Cultural Imagination in Nineteenth-Century Paris*, Oxford: Oxford University Press, 2009.

Ham, Anthony, *Lonely Planet: Madrid*, London: Lonely Planet Publications, 2013.

Hazan, Eric, *The Invention of Paris: A History in Footsteps*, London, Verso, 2011.

Hemingway, Ernest, *Death in the Afternoon* (1932), New York: Simon & Schuster, 2014.

Hooper, John, *The New Spaniards*, London: Penguin, 2006.

Hussey, Andrew, *Paris: The Secret History*, London: Bloomsbury, 2007.

Ingold, Tim & Vergunst, Jo Lee, *Ways of Walking: Ethnography and Practice on Foot*, London: Routledge, 2008.

Jacobs, Michael, *Madrid Observed*, London: Pallas Athene, 2006.

Kapuscinski, Ryszard, *The Other*, London: Verso, 2008.

Lorca, Federico García, *Gypsy Ballads* (trans. Jane Durán), London: Enitharmon Press.

--------------, *Sketches of Spain* (trans. Peter Bush), London, Serif, 2012.

Mathieson, David, *Frontline Madrid: Battlefield Tours of the Spanish Civil War*, Oxford: Signal Books, 2014.

Max, D.T., *The Family That Couldn't Sleep: A Medical Mystery*, New York: Random House, 2007.

Menocal, María Rosa, *The Ornament of the World: How Muslims, Jews, and Christians Created a Culture of Tolerance in Medieval Spain*, London: Little, Brown, 2003.

Muecke, Stephen, *Contingency in Madagascar*, Bristol: Intellect Books, 2012.

Muro, Veronica Ramírez, *Secret Madrid*, Versailles: Jonglez Publishing, 2011.

Nash, Elizabeth, *Madrid: A Cultural and Literary History*, Oxford: Signal Books, 2001.

Rousseau, Jean-Jacques, *Emile: or, On Education* (1762) (trans. A. Bloom), Basic Books, 1979.

-----------, *Reveries of the Solitary Walker* (1782) (trans. Russell Goulbourne), Oxford: Oxford University Press, 2011)

Said, Edward, *Orientalism*, New York: Vintage Books, 1979.

Sandhu, Sukhdev, 2010 *Night Haunts: A Journey Through the London Night*, London: Verso, 2010.

Shaya, Gregory, "The *Flâneur*, the *Badaud*, and the Making of a Mass Public in France, circa 1860-1910", *American Historical Review* 109 (1), 2004.

Stewart, Jules, *Madrid: The History*, London: I.B. Tauris, 2012.

Thompson, C.W., *French Romantic Travel Writing: Chateaubriand to Nerval*,

Oxford: Oxford University Press, 2011.

Tremlett, Giles, *Ghosts of Spain: Travels Through a Country's Hidden Past*, London: Faber & Faber, 2012.

Twain, Mark *The Innocents Abroad* (1869), Ware: Wordsworth Editions, 2010.

Urry, John, *The Tourist Gaze*, London: Sage, 2002.

Valle-Inclán, Ramón María del, *Luces de Bohemia* (1920), Barcelona: Espasa-Calpe, 1992.

Wilentz, Amy, "The Role of the Literary Journalist in the Digital Era". *Literary Journalism Studies*, 6 (2), 31-42, 2014.

Withey, Lynne, *Grand Tours and Cook's Tours: A History of Leisure Travel 1750-1915*, London: Aurum Press 1997.

Wordsworth, William, *The Poems of William Wordsworth*, Penrith: Humanities-Ebooks, 2009.

Youngs, Tim, " Interview with William Dalrymple". *Studies in Travel Writing*, 9 (1), 2005.